EDWARD SKLOOT

SO-AXB-358

Beyond the Money

REFLECTIONS ON PHILANTHROPY,
THE NONPROFIT SECTOR
AND CIVIC LIFE, 1999-2006

THE SURDNA FOUNDATION
NEW YORK

ISBN: 978-0-9795814-0-3

Library of Congress number: 2007903010

Printed in the United States of America.
All materials and processes used in producing
this report are environmentally responsible.
The cover paper is Domtar Proterra, made from
40% post-consumer fiber. The text paper is
Mohawk Via, made from 100% post-consumer
fiber and manufactured using wind-generated
electricity. The inks used for printing are
vegetable oil-based. This report is fully recyclable.
When recycling, place with mixed papers.

For additional copies of this book, please contact
The Surdna Foundation.

Edward Skloot can be reached at ed@skloot.com.

Editor: Tony Proscio
Design: Landesberg Design

The Surdna Foundation
330 Madison Avenue, 30th Floor
New York, NY 10017
tel (212) 557-0010
www.surdna.org

To Suzanne and Joe

Table of Contents

Introduction
A look back, and forward   I

CHAPTER I
From Purpose to Power   5
A critical look at American philanthropy,
and some reasons for hope

     from Moving from Satisfaction to Significance   6

     from Slot Machines, Boat Building and the
     Future of Philanthropy   17

     from Is Distinguished Philanthropy
     Still Possible?   34

     from Doing Better—It Isn't About
     the Money   46

CHAPTER 2
Higher Values, Bottom Lines   61
The future of the nonprofit sector
in the Age of Enterprise

     from Twenty-Five Years of Social
     Entrepreneurship in Twenty-Five Minutes   62

     from The Nonprofit Sector and the Market:
     Challenges and Opportunities   75

     Should Foundation Officers Serve on
     Their Grantees' Boards?   89

CHAPTER 3

'To Strengthen the Bonds Among Us'   97
Thoughts on nurturing civil society,
citizenship and the public sphere

    from Philanthropy's Role in Building
    an Effective Citizenry   98

    from Hyperbole, Shrinking Budgets
    and Government Devolution   116

    from Let's Face the Music and Dance   123

    from A Citizen's Oath for America   129

Index   135

Introduction

A look back, and forward

What you have in your hands is a kind of walking tour through several critical concerns facing philanthropy, the nonprofit sector and civil society. The concerns were put forth in a number of talks I was honored to give over the last eight years, of which these are a representative selection. Taken together, they are one person's effort to define, analyze, make sense of and suggest remedies to challenges that beset civic organizations specifically created for our collective betterment.

The impetus for the publication was the ongoing flow of requests for copies of individual speeches. Sometimes, too, colleagues would mention the usefulness of one or another of these talks in puzzling out the dilemmas they faced in the sector. It seemed to me that the demand for copies (despite their being posted on the Surdna Foundation website) was uncommonly high, and therefore that a printed compilation might be worth putting in the public domain. The board of directors of the Surdna Foundation agreed with this conclusion and graciously underwrote the costs of editing and publication.

I hope these talks (and one memo) will be a spark for further thought, investigation and debate, as well as a spur to colleagues to implement some of the changes suggested. For example, the paucity of useful research data, the lack of effective sectoral and cross-sectoral collaborations, and the pathetic level of advocacy by foundations all can be changed if we choose to. In fact, if we want to boost the influence of our sector, then we'll have to work more empathetically, more energetically, more politically.

Only this year has the field seen an excellent, comprehensive text on the history of and current issues facing philanthropy—by Joel L. Fleishman, in *The Foundation: A Great American Secret*. The little collection you are reading now is wider in its scope and more impressionistic in its tone than Joel's finely honed, expert review of the philanthropic sector. But I hope this contribution will also be provocative and useful. Call it the "sorbet course" in an ongoing dinner conversation about the uncommon challenges facing civil society.

This book is being published to mark the conclusion of my 18 years as CEO of the Surdna Foundation (1989–2007). In this time, philanthropy has slowly moved toward center stage in defining and solving national and international problems. Since the burst of the technology bubble in 2001, philanthropy's growth has revived and has been huge — both in the number of foundations created and in the amount of money spent in mission-related activities. As long as the economy holds reasonably strong, we can expect this growth to continue. Thus, the bigger challenges before us can be met with more money, hopefully (as described in this book) delivered in more effective ways.

The Surdna board (and the larger Andrus family) gave me the opportunity to think about many of our most important challenges, as well as the authority to act on them. The board has been central to all successes I have had, and its commitment to raising the level of philanthropic excellence has been both sustained and exceptional. I am grateful to them and feel honored to have worked for them. Our staff has worked at the highest level of skill and compassion, and they have been, along with our grantee—colleagues, my teachers and friends. All have had a piece of these speeches, though only I am responsible for their content. I hope they pass muster and that the ideas behind them will provoke continuous discussion and relentless action.

— Edward Skloot
May 2007

I

From Purpose
to Power

A critical look at
American philanthropy,
and some reasons for hope

These remarks were delivered four months after the passing of John W. Gardner, a titan of philanthropy whose later years were devoted to building a vigorous, courageous and visionary Third Sector in the United States—a cause that his many books on the subject continue to advance.

from

Moving from Satisfaction to Significance

Keynote address to The Donors' Forum annual meeting, Chicago, Illinois, June 20, 2002.

What would you do if suddenly you had $100 million, or $1 billion, to build a foundation on?

What would you do? What if there were no strings attached concerning focus or direction or style, no limits on place or population, no rules about big grants or small, lots of staff or just a few, much visibility or complete anonymity? What would you do?

What would you do if you had no relatives, no creditors, no obligations, no guilt, no political constraints, no board of directors?

What would you do?

If you already work in philanthropy, would you do more of the same, a lot more, in the program areas where you now spend your time? Or would

6

you try something very different? Would you simplify the work processes? Speed up the decision processes? Raise salaries? Think really big? Take the money and run? What would you do?

This question is for real. At a minimum it can help us look at ourselves in the mirror. We can then make some crucial distinctions about how to do our best work. Take a moment, sit quietly, maybe close your eyes. ...What would you do?

What would you do if *you* had $1 billion and no string, no rules, no obligations?

One thing *I'd* do is look for precedent. Did I have an ancestor, or two, whose thoughts I could excavate and learn from? Could I dig up the jaw bone or the hip of an early philanthropoid and compose its story? I tried. I went back in time and found three of special note: John D. Rockefeller, Andrew Carnegie and Julius Rosenwald.[1]

These ancestors, founders of the *field* of philanthropy, were great individuals. They acted boldly, grandly and often alone. They didn't love government but learned to work with it or around it. Rockefeller, in fact, originally tried to set up his foundation for the federal government to control and virtually run, but he was rebuffed by a suspicious Congress.

Of course, they lived and worked in a different time and place. But they are important, in my view, because, first, they tell us to take on "root causes" and, second, to stick with them for the long haul. They created fields and institutions that never before existed. They used their imagination and money to

7

do what philanthropists must do: make social change.

What did *they* do? Carnegie and Rockefeller, the two "Robber Barons," were also the greatest philanthropists in American history.

Rockefeller created, among other initiatives, the General Education Board. It revolutionized higher and public education in America, especially in the South. He virtually created the fields of public health and medical research, which eradicated hookworm, then yellow fever and malaria. And, of course, along the way he founded the University of Chicago, Rockefeller University and more.

Carnegie donated 1,700 public libraries across the country. Since local communities had to provide the land and perpetual maintenance, as well as the books, this was probably the first example in philanthropy of large-scale "matching grants." The tie-in with local communities probably qualifies as an early version of "public–private partnerships," too. Carnegie set up an insurance company to provide pensions for teachers, all of whom at the time were horribly underpaid. Today the company has morphed into TIAA-CREF.

Julius Rosenwald fought for racial and social justice. The Jewish founder of Sears, Roebuck & Co. built dozens of YMCAs and YWCAs across the country. He contributed to the construction of 5,300 schools, workshops and teachers' homes in 833 counties in 15 southern states. He made local governments deed the land forever. They had to put up two-thirds of the cost through tax levy money to assure African Americans their education. This was another remarkable public–private partnership.

After World War I it was said that 60 percent of African Americans who had completed primary school had been educated at a Rosenwald school.

Our forebears lived in a different era, and they were well-built for that age. They knew what to do. In their age of rationalism and "scientific philan-thropy," they believed that analysis and expertise, coupled with comprehensive efforts, could solve "root cause" problems. *That* was philanthropy.

Can we pick up on their grand enterprise and extend it further? I think the answer is "yes," but first we have to get our bearings and clear out some of the underbrush of modern philanthropy.

Our forebears coupled expertise with comprehensive reforms to tackle 'root causes.' That was philanthropy.

Turning Philanthropy Outside-In

The first step is to challenge a way of working that gets us all in a lot of trouble. Philanthropic advisors start the conversation by asking potential (or actual) donors, "What is your passion?" From there they help generate programs for giving. This approach lies at the heart of American philanthropy, both personal and institutional. It's the individualistic, anything-goes style where almost no idea, however smart or foolish, is scrutinized by others. Did you have a great kindergarten teacher? Work on early childhood education! Did you deliver newspapers? Try entrepreneurship!

9

The International House of Pancakes Theory of Philanthropy: Lots of good works stack up into a tower of effectiveness.

You get the point. The question is asked from the inside out: What is *your* passion? It invariably focuses on individual donor satisfaction first—and only then on the significance of the action.

Our three philanthropic ancestors seem to me to have worked from the outside in. They first asked, "What is needed?" and put their considerable money and talent into crafting the answer. They *were* engaged. But they also analyzed "root causes," and got lots of professional help to understand core problems.

This focus on stoking individual passion in grantmaking props up an unwritten assumption: what I call the International House of Pancakes Theory of Philanthropy. The IHOP Theory says this: Lots of good works, irrespective of felt need, but earnestly sprinkled about, will stack up into a great tower of philanthropic effectiveness. It bears little connection to reality.

For example, in mid-2002 the Annenberg Challenge, the $1.1 billion, eight-year effort to improve beleaguered schools, issued its own faintly damning report. The largest national experiment ever tried—in 2,400 schools in 18 sites—acknowledged the lack of dramatic gains. It said, "The challenge did not work miracles, but it breathed life into American education.... It brought hope to schools that had been all but abandoned.[2] One-point-one billion dollars is a lot of money to pay for hope. I know there were individual success stories in some schools and sites. But I also wonder whether even successful programs will have much to show for the effort in the long haul.

In fact, today we have philanthropic *sprawl* in every area of giving. All ships do not rise, certainly not all the ones that need raising. We know this. But the "don't ask, don't tell" approach to grant-making is guaranteed to produce little useful data and few transferable lessons. More often than not, successes are isolated, unconnected and transitory.

With no barriers to entry and an absence of much hard, shareable data, it's easy to see why philanthropy has a hard time improving *systematically*. Ultimately, our success as a field depends on mapping all of our efforts, and the government's, on articulating our "theories of change," and on holding programs up for sharing and scrutiny by our peers.

A great example of mapping—literally—has been taking place in Philadelphia. There, the Reinvestment Fund, working with philanthropic dollars, has just mapped virtually every important market-related component in every local neighborhood: from tax delinquency to vacant land, from abandoned housing to abandoned cars. Now, working with Mayor John Street, they have categorized every single neighborhood into six objective, data-driven tiers, from "Regional Choice" to "Reclamation." With these maps, Philadelphia can finally begin to develop targeted reinvestment strategies for each community and

Today we have philanthropic *sprawl* in every area of giving.

allocate scarce resources effectively.

BLURRING THE BOUNDARIES

A second task, besides focusing on real needs and developing and using hard data, is to break down program silos. That way we can deal with each other more productively.

The sector, like intelligence-gathering at the FBI or CIA, often works in stovepipes of specialists. Interactivity is resisted. In fact, it's an undeveloped skill. Youth experts don't deal much with school reformers; social workers with job developers; economic development professionals with community organizers. Almost no one talks with artists. How can we connect program dots?

Each of us sincerely seeks to put our own stake in the ground and make it as effective as possible. But individual, unconnected good works run counter to continuous learning and collaboration. Absent these, our work won't mirror the complexity of the real world or help us develop comprehensive, wise solutions.

That's what makes Chicago's Fund for Immigrants and Refugees so notable. Twenty-seven organizations over five years raised more than $7 million to tackle post-welfare-reform immigrant needs: legal, economic, social. The final report tells a wonderful story about the values—and uniqueness—of a collaboration that worked together, learned together, leveraged each other and treated

The sector, like intelligence-gathering at the FBI or CIA, often works in stovepipes of specialists.

all organizations with speed and respect. Philanthropy and the State of Illinois came together and
met a challenge inherent in the Welfare Reform
Act. Fine job. Fine model.

What would you do if you could do something like it?

There are other, national examples to suggest
how powerful working together can be. For example, in 1992 the Surdna Foundation sparked the
Comprehensive Community Revitalization Program.
A dozen funders poured over $30 million and
much technical assistance into five CDCs in the
South Bronx. This effort had a lot to do with the
stunning revival of that poster child of urban decay.

To do philanthropy
well is to do it
collaboratively.

Working together is much harder than going it
alone. The management of the process can be
tough. Joint learning can be haphazard. Egos can be
fragile. Sometimes the work can sink to the lowest
common denominator. But I would argue that
to do philanthropy well is to *do it collaboratively*, to
learn together, to share vital information together,
possibly to fund together and to evaluate together.
This applies to foundations. It also applies to nonprofits. And to funders and nonprofits together.
When done right, it's also a lot of fun.

Of course not all work need be, or should be,
done in partnership. But so much more can be
accomplished by aggregating our power and expertise it amazes me how unusual it is.

I have to emphasize that collaborations need to

avoid the IHOP Theory, too. If they are set up to please funders only, or they ignore the needs and expertise of nonprofits, they will never get under way smartly. They will continue to evoke nervousness among nonprofit organizations, who are nervous enough already.

The final reason for doing collaborative work is recognition that our resources are finite and the needs are great. While grantmaking doubled in the last half of the last decade, it still comprised a small fraction of the real need. If we stay isolated and fly solo, we simply won't have enough fuel to accomplish our philanthropic job of social change.

Even though it's legal, advocacy gives some foundations the willies.

FINDING OUR VOICE

All this leads directly to the third idea: that big intentions and strategic collaborations must be backed up by *advocacy*—lots of it. In our field, support for advocacy is truly rare. Even though it's legal, foundations get the willies when the subject comes up. Some boards are sometimes shocked—shocked!— at the suggestion that they actually do such a thing. Picking up the signal, some nonprofits stare at their shoe tops and abjectly deny that such a thing could ever happen.

With all our great financial success and even prominence, much of our sector is remarkably quiet on such basic matters as growing economic inequality, civil rights and poverty alleviation.

Recall the passing of John Gardner. The former

head of the Carnegie Corporation, Secretary of Health, Education and Welfare, and founder of Common Cause died in February 2002. His death took from us the last voice of conscience and responsible prodding our field could claim as its own. Gardner raised his voice for an engaged, responsive, participatory civic sector. Where are the other John Gardners? Those who can weigh in on the side of citizen and philanthropic activism? Those who see the positive value of positive government? Where have we been on such matters as repealing the estate tax, assuring health care for 40 million uncovered Americans and maintaining stronger safety nets?

Now think about Paul Ylvisaker, the most incisive thinker in our field, who died ten years before John Gardner. He once spoke of the "weak identity and self image of foundations and of the third sector generally." Back in 1977 he said:

> There is little sense of presence, not as much as some of our prose would indicate. When public criticism mounts and attacks begin, we don't bark very loud, and I guess it may be because nobody feels our bite. But I think it may be even more because of public uncertainty over who we are.[3]

What would Gardner and Ylvisaker do? I think they would demand we speak out loudly and compassionately for the values we represent, with the data and the expertise we have developed to back it up.

They would absolutely applaud the recent work

Gardner and Ylvisaker would demand that we speak out loudly and compassionately for the values we represent.

If we don't use our collective power of persuasion, as well as our money, to set the policy table, who will?

on national welfare reform pulled together by the Joyce Foundation. As you know, 24 studies covering seven Midwestern states were assembled to show how reform had been started—but that many former welfare recipients were still mired in poverty. They argued that it was time to enhance the safety net, not tear it full of bigger holes.[4]

This advocacy was well prepared and well timed. It made all the major media. It woke up many Congressmen and their committees. It probably guaranteed that, next time, the Joyce Foundation, and others, would be asked for input. There's always a slice of good luck when advocacy hits the bull's eye, but we can't make our weight felt unless we step on the scale. Or, as a Zen-friend of mine likes to say, "Everything in life is an accident, but there are ways to make yourself accident-prone."

We simply have to find our voice. If we don't speak for the civic good, who will? If we don't use our collective power of persuasion, as well as our money, to set the policy table, who will? Ylvisaker told philanthropy not to forget its "moral thermostat that flips when we are confronted by suffering, injustice, inequality or callous behavior."[5] Rockefeller, Carnegie and Rosenwald would surely agree.

Most of these thoughts (with some later additions and editing) were presented at what has become an annual Georgetown symposium honoring the memory of Wally Nielsen, the most prominent commentator on philanthropy (and one of its keener critics) in the late 20th century. If this look at philanthropy seems harsh— and I don't really think it is—it is nonetheless relatively mild compared with Wally's sharpest comments on our field.

The seminar took place just one month after the horror of September 11, 2001, a coincidence noted near the end of the speech.

from

Slot Machines, Boat Building and the Future of Philanthropy

Among its various departments and programs, the United States Conference of Catholic Bishops has an officer with the awesome title "Secretary of Social Development and World Peace." John Carr, who has borne the humbling weight of that job description for well over a decade, tells of an incident at the bishops' annual meeting some years ago, when he stepped onto a hotel elevator wearing his identification badge—name and title. A woman passenger on the elevator, noting that he did not seem to be a clergyman, asked what his role was

Inaugural address to the Waldemar A. Nielsen Issues in Philanthropy Seminar, Georgetown University, Washington, D.C., October 5, 2001.

with the Bishops' Conference. Drawing her attention to his name tag, he read off his official title.

As the woman stepped off the elevator, she looked back at him indulgently and said, "Can you please do a little better?"

Well, shouldn't we ask the same of philanthropy? We don't have to hold ourselves responsible for World Peace . . . but couldn't we be doing a little better?

BIG HOPES, SMALL CHANGE

If we're honest, we'd have to start with the premise that much of the way philanthropy does its business is dysfunctional. Sometimes it actually sabotages the best work in the field. Often it leaves a lot of hard feelings behind, too. Despite the good works of individual funders, overall, the system is broken.

Think about modern American philanthropy: We're like gamblers playing the two-dollar slots in Vegas. We sit bolt upright, holding our little bucket of metal coins. Repeatedly, we drop in small change, hoping for a big payoff. We face straight ahead, rarely pulling our eyes away from the spinning icons. We don't interact with the other players on our left or right. If we did, we wouldn't learn much anyhow. They're behaving in just the same way.

Essentially, we put small coins on large dreams. Even if we win a modest jackpot, we almost always feed the slots more than we win. We may be "up" for a while. But most likely we're down, and vaguely uneasy at the end of each cycle. "It just

We're like gamblers playing the two-dollar slots in Vegas. Repeatedly, we drop in small change, hoping for a big payoff.

wasn't our day." Our exit strategy is the EXIT sign.

Much of philanthropy, especially at the 100 largest foundations, with perhaps half the field's endowment, works in isolation, rarely sharing the task or the results. We make grants based on inadequate due diligence, partially relevant information or simple intuition. After a grant is made we rarely share what we really know—the good, the bad and the ugly—with grantees or with our colleagues. We are novices at cross-program, cross-sector collaboration and rarely buddy-up for mutual gain. In fact, there are no incentives in philanthropy to do that. Finally, we don't usually measure our successes, course-correct and learn intentionally.

> We rarely share what we really know—the good, the bad and the ugly—with grantees or with our colleagues.

Of course, not all foundations behave like this, at all times, with all grantees and colleagues. This is a description of the overall *system*[6] of philanthropy, and here are the system's rules of the road. They speak volumes about who we are.

Primarily, our work focuses on grantmaking. Grants are made on the basis of proposals. The submission requirements are sometimes over-detailed and arduous. The time it takes for funders to consider and disburse grants varies, from very quick to nearly endless. Communications from program staff, and even senior executives, may be unclear. Foundations (as well as individual givers and corporations) have different filing requirements, deadlines, time frames and grant sizes, so nonprofits have to do some really fancy footwork to get by. Every year they are compelled to cobble together their operating (and capital) budgets from numerous, quite unconnected, quite idiosyncratic sources of capital.

This makes raising capital highly labor-intensive. It bends nonprofit executives away from focusing on strategy and operations. We all know that, sometimes, in order to start new programs, or keep old ones alive, nonprofits "adjust" their programs and chase the scarce foundation dollar.

It is absolutely true that some individual funders communicate and relate to grantees better than others. But philanthropy's operating system is full of potholes, hidden curves and soft shoulders. What may appear rational to individual funders may, collectively, be nearly unworkable for grant-seekers. Further, philanthropy effectively throws nearly all responsibility onto the grant-seeker while retaining for itself the right to make and alter the rules. One social service executive recently bemoaned that he sometimes feels like Tom Hanks storming the beach in *Saving Private Ryan*.

For example, it's commonly agreed that funders have been cutting back on general-support grants. They increasingly tilt toward project support and let grantees absorb overhead costs. This approach makes nonprofits increasingly unstable by denying reimbursement for their core expenses. It has led to persistent, though often muted, protests by nonprofits. This pushback has made little difference in philanthropy. It hasn't even generated sustained conversation.

Philanthropy effectively throws nearly all responsibility onto the grant-seeker while retaining for itself the right to make and alter the rules.

20

Sometimes funders create their own approaches. They start entirely new institutions in a deliberate attempt to change the playing field. Sometimes this is necessary. Yet it often has the effect of stoking mistrust, or fear, among grantees who may have come (at least partially) to rely on their support.

Is Every Choice a Short Straw?

OK. Let's assume the nonprofit is successful in navigating the rules of the road. It advances literacy or develops lots of job placements, or builds affordable housing or improves community safety. Even where success is achieved, more funding may still not result. Grantmaking can be so unpredictable.

For some funders, apparent success provides the opportunity to walk away and do something else. No reward here. For others, success leads to the reverse situation: increased funding. At times, these funders, correctly or not, urge nonprofits to expand their programs, or to replicate them in other places. This push to "go to scale" is not regularly accompanied by ample capital to do the expanded job that funders encourage. When this happens, it exacerbates the undercapitalization of nonprofits and sometimes makes the nonprofit weaker, not stronger.

On the other hand, for some funders, it is *failure* that provides reason to continue funding. They think more money, time and effort would deliver the desired results. For still others, success or failure may be irrelevant. For unrelated reasons, they decide the time has come to alter their guidelines and head for the exit. As an added twist, and all too frequently, large grants from a big funder signal others to shy away; they conclude that the first foundation "owns" the program and are reluctant to take a second position.

A very successful grantee of Surdna's e-mailed me this a few years ago:

> We are so 'scarcity constrained' that we typically tout whatever we are up to as The Cure for What Ails. We are worried that if we don't oversell our particular solution, then some other organization that does oversell will get the modicum of available support. And this is all such a slippery slope because nonprofits that oversell can't deliver... funders that have invested in what they believe to be a macro solution are disappointed by tiny incremental gains... clients/end users get partially served and fully frustrated... and the vicious cycle is perpetuated.[7]

In these funding decisions, the effectiveness of grantees seems to have little relevance. Peter Frumkin and Mark Kim of Harvard's Kennedy School of Government recently studied nonprofits in many fields over an 11-year period. They found that "nonprofits that position themselves as cost-efficient—reporting low administrative-to-total expense ratios—fared no better over time than less efficient-appearing organizations in the market for individual, foundation, and corporate contributions."[8]

Large grants from a big funder signal others to shy away; they conclude that the first foundation 'owns' the program.

The same conclusion has been reached by Jed Emerson, an economic development expert who has been a senior advisor to the Hewlett Foundation. His pioneering studies of grantmaking and social investing are sharply critical of the foundation–grantee "dance."[9] Outcomes, he says, are rarely important in the decision to fund or to re-up for another round.

Finally, numerous funders are unclear about what kinds of funds may be available. They may not be frank about whether they provide startup funds, bridge funds, long-term support or capacity-building grants. Sometimes there is little clear signaling about *how much* capital may be available, and the decision may take many months to find out. So funders continually upend grantees' expectations. Often they come through with smaller-than-antic-ipated grants. Occasionally they give more than asked for. The result, *system-wide*, is the massive undercapitalization of nonprofits due to widespread fragmentation of effort, poorly targeted dollars and inadequate communication bordering on secrecy.

While some might argue that this "let-a-thousand-flowers-bloom" approach is inherently democratic, normal and typically American, I suggest that it is autocratic, ineffective and willful—and typically American. Philanthropy certainly doesn't build toward Prof. Robert Putnam's definition of *social capital*: "Social networks and the norms of reci-procity and trustworthiness that arise from them."[10]

The result, *system-wide*, is the massive undercapitalization of nonprofits.

DOLING ALONE

We have just come off an era of enormous philanthropic expansion. Most philanthropies compiled very strong returns in the 1990s, some well into double-digits annually. Surdna's own endowment more than doubled, and we gave out $250 million, too. The '90s were philanthropy's big chance to discuss the rules of the road, experiment with new processes, improve communications, build relationships with grantees and find genuine common cause among funders. Yet the surge of money, old and newly minted, doesn't seem to have fundamentally improved the way the system functions. Nor does it seem to have made service delivery more effective.

> The surge of money, old and newly minted, doesn't seem to have fundamentally improved the way the system functions.

Why do we act this way? Surely a lot has to do with deeply rooted behavior patterns: This is the way it's always been done.

Then there is the single-minded individualism of philanthropy, going all the way back to Rockefeller and Carnegie. Funders just don't see their work systemically, as part of a whole. For example, until recently we saw no need for a newspaper to cover philanthropy and nonprofits, and, after a buoyant decade, we still have only one bi-monthly. Serious research is still a rarity; research relevant to the broad interests of the sector is even more rare.

Our trade association seems to scrupulously avoid taking up hard, key issues, like the estate tax. Only a small handful of funders make grants in the field of philanthropy and nonprofit organizations, and the number is not growing.

Finally, in philanthropy there's no need to be externally accountable, and no sanction from the marketplace, so there's virtually no incentive to improve, individually or as a group.

It doesn't have to be this way. We can learn to collaborate among ourselves and with our grantees and, as they say, "leverage" one another.

One small ray of hope comes from "funding collaboratives." These are joint ventures among groups of like-minded philanthropies. The largest and most notable is the National Community Development Initiative (NCDI). More than a dozen foundations, banks, insurance companies and HUD participate. NCDI has been in operation for a decade. It has disbursed more than $250 million in grants and concessionary loans to CDCs in 23 cities (through the Local Initiatives Support Corporation and the Enterprise Foundation). Another effort is the Los Angeles Urban Funders Group. It began seven years ago and now embraces almost 30 funders and corporations. It has put more than $6 million into improving three local neighborhoods. Excellent work is now occurring in the broader environmental field, too, in sustainable forestry, climate change and toxics.

A related example is the Funders Network on Smart Growth and Livable Communities. It uses information instead of grants to leverage impact.

One small ray of hope comes from 'funding collaboratives.'

We should be
more skeptical
about the much
discussed 'venture
philanthropy.'

In a little over two years it has attracted 60 foundations of all sizes and dozens of nonprofit affiliates.
It has created a truly comprehensive website, accessible to both funders and nonprofits, to share what
they know. Its small secretariat champions group
learning and sponsors cross-sectoral research.
The research connects such disparate areas as aging,
public health and educational access to smart
growth practices.

At their best, collaboratives change the rules of
the road. They make grantmaking more predictable
and supportive of grantees. They harmonize goals,
processes and phasing. They offer the chance for a
group of funders to proceed at the same time from
an agreed-upon, common platform. This reduces
the mystery of grantmaking. It adds regularity and
consistency and sometimes a focus on outcomes.
It brings funders and grantees into a more engaged,
collegial relationship. The parts start to work
adaptively, together.

As yet, there aren't many funding collaboratives
and they tend to be seriously undercapitalized.
They could be more effective, too. Seldom are they
at the top of the agenda of most funders; everyone
wants to play the slots with a little money and still
get a big payoff. Large dreams follow small coins.

We should be more skeptical about the
much discussed "venture philanthropy." While the
arrangement is often claimed to be a partnership,
focusing on organizational and financial improvement,

we haven't yet seen enough of it to draw any conclusions. If this hybrid form of philanthropy invests its money well, strengthens institutions, creates incentives for organizational performance with more money and develops mutually helpful metrics, then it has much promise. Yet some investees may not be up to the task—and neither might the venture philanthropists, particularly if they expect results too quickly.

We will never decisively improve the field until we learn to deal with each other more collegially and trustingly.

LESSONS FROM THE BOATYARD

If strong funding collaboratives can help to improve inter-foundation giving, what will improve the rules governing grantor–grantee relationships? Obviously, I am very concerned about this. I believe a "cultural" shift must occur in the system. Both funders and nonprofits need to consciously build social capital. We will never decisively improve the field of philanthropy until we learn to deal with each other more collegially and trustingly. Yes, power relationships will never entirely disappear. But they certainly can be altered. Here are three steps we need to take:

1. A Field of Shared Meaning. First is to intentionally create what MIT systems theorist Peter Senge calls a "field of shared meaning."[11] This begins with creating a reflective, safe environment, where funders and nonprofit executives can discuss their concerns over relationships, policies and strategies. Individual visions and styles can be affirmed or altered. This will be hard to do—as hard for nonprofits as for funders. Both would need to find common, honest language and be willing to drop their protective armor.

Those with power should act first, possibly by joining with nonprofits to promulgate a "Code of Pretty Good Behavior" that can be mutually monitored and constantly upgraded. They could track, scrutinize and assess the grantmaking rules-of-the-road. They could trace what works and what doesn't, and even prepare an annual report card, a kind of Zagat guide to the best and worst of the field.

2. Mapping the System. A second step is mapping the programs and all the "money flows" in each field, like arts or education or human services, in specific geographical areas. The money flows would include corporate and government dollars, too. This is seldom done,[12] causing redundant or ineffective grantmaking. An obvious case is in the field of educational reform in numerous cities. Here, more philanthropic and corporate money has been spent, less effectively and more idiosyncratically, than in any field I know. Constantly mapping the system will tell us an awful lot about how the whole field interacts, changes and innovates. It will give a common baseline. We must compile these maps to help us to chart improved program and financing strategies, and we must share widely the information we derive.

Those with power should act first to promulgate a 'Code of Pretty Good Behavior' that can be mutually monitored.

3. Co-Creating Value. Which brings me to my third proposal, "co-creating" value, as seen in the example of boat-building.

Two business school professors at the University of Michigan wrote a very provocative paper some time ago, describing how manufacturers and customers work together with high trust and big results.[13] They highlight the impressive story of innovation in boat-building that occurs in, of all places, landlocked rural Kentucky.

Sumerset Houseboats, the world's largest houseboat manufacturer, engages in "co-creating value." What is co-created is not only the boat. That's the physical artifact. It is also a *process*, where boat buyers engage in continuous waves of interaction with the manufacturer. The two also build a relationship. The customer has access to the accumulated data of other buyers, as well as the company's resident experts. There is a high level of transparency from beginning to end, from configuration to design, from manufacturing to testing. Engineers and carpenters share what they know. All are involved in a continuous dialogue.

In the words of the two professors who wrote the study, the old boat-building process is transformed. It moves from "own and extract value *from* the consumer" to "respect, dialogue and co-creation of value *with* the consumer" (italics added). The former power of the supplier is transformed to the *greater* power of the two together.

'Co-creating value' is a process where buyers and builders engage in continuous waves of interaction.

29

The authors add: "Sumerset is an illustration of a system where the entire order-to-delivery process is transparent, accessible, invites dialogue, and offers opportunities to explicitly recognize risks."[14]

Further, "there is a significant 'forgetting' element here. Managers must come to terms with the genetic code of their organizations and develop explicit strategies for moving the entire organization to the new ways in which values will be created."[15]

If I wanted a houseboat, you know who I'd buy from. The quality of the experience and of the final product would convince me, hands down. I'd not only get a great new boat, I'd get a partner, helper and teacher, too. Sounds a lot like social capital to me.

Needless to say, in both boat-building and philanthropy, co-creation of value isn't easy to accomplish. In fact, in our field it's not clear who is the supplier and who is the consumer. Are funders the sellers and nonprofits the buyers? Or do nonprofits sell and funders buy? That the lines are blurred in our field seems to suggest that co-creation of value is trickier to accomplish, but no less important to try.

In our field, co-creation of value is trickier to accomplish than in commercial boat-building, but no less important to try.

There is a tremendous need here for sophisticated use of information technology. Quick feedback loops are necessary in order to course-correct. Knowledge becomes as important as money. There is a need to provide incentives for grantmakers to "forget" their old ways. They have to see the value in working jointly and respectfully with grantees to "build their boat together." The manufacturer and the consumer, the grantor and the grantee, have to recognize that they are two inseparable sides of the same coin.

More than funders, foundations become information resources, brokers, learners and listeners, and promoters of success.

PHILANTHROPY AS CO-CREATION

So, look at it this way. Suppose we didn't use money as our primary vehicle for getting and measuring results. Suppose grants aren't just discrete transactions made in linear fashion, where if you meet the goals you get more money. That's a 19th-century model: mechanistic, transactional and isolating.

Suppose a new model, more like a network. It has several operating characteristics. It is driven by information and knowledge, which are shared constantly and purposefully among grantees and foundations, by web, print and constant personal connection. Relationships flourish. Mutual learning occurs. Technical assistance is constant. Metrics aid accountability, but they are determined jointly and shared jointly for mutual gain.

Under this model, the foundations' role needs to be re-imagined. Instead of funders, they become information resources, brokers (and givers) of money and relationships, ongoing learners and listeners, and active promoters of success. They are enablers of improvement and resources to connect to. In fact, even when the stock market sinks, their larger repertoire can help moderate the damage brought on by reduced funding. The multiple roles funders fulfill will help them maintain the effort more effectively.

One consequence of this new concept of philanthropy would be to review the numbers of program staff and their talents. The role of the program officer shifts, as does the CEO's. Their knowledge of the field, their maturity and their ability to collaborate become easily as important as their ability to analyze grant proposals. This shift, in turn, could lead to a review of the costs of staff relative to administrative overhead. Under a more embracing concept of its work, more money might need to go for more staff, performing a more comprehensive, relationship- and information-focused job.

What, then, could philanthropy be?

I can imagine a system embracing ongoing, positive partnerships, among funders, among nonprofits and between them. They would work together under open, *mutually* agreed-upon and adaptable rules. The rules would be geared toward producing successful outcomes by sharing useful information, by learning together, by treating each other respectfully, by encouraging and using feedback, by leveraging resources from all the sectors. If we look inside ourselves and across the field, I think we can discern this great opportunity and great challenge. In fact, in the wake of the terrorist action on September 11, we can also see that the

The rules would be geared toward sharing useful information, learning together, leveraging resources from all the sectors.

world—and philanthropy's role, no less—will never be the same. At this moment of tremendous discontinuity, we will do ourselves a disservice if we neglect the opportunity to reform, or to transform, our philanthropic ways.

In the older style of transactional philanthropy, the wheel is still turning but the gerbil is on its last legs. I deeply believe that the time has come to re-imagine our system of relationships and processes, and our goals, in order to move philanthropy to a more synergistic, creative and effective next phase. This is the task before us. None of us alone knows how to do it. But together, we can co-create our future.

In the older style of transactional philanthropy, the wheel is still turning but the gerbil is on its last legs.

These remarks contribute to a long, rich and ongoing discussion in Minnesota about the characteristics of outstanding philanthropy. The Minnesota Council on Foundations has itself contributed valuably to this discussion by publishing a list of eight 'Principles for Minnesota Grantmakers,' a document whose implications reach well beyond that state. In that spirit, these comments are both national and local in scope, applicable practically anywhere, but with examples and inspiration from the good work under way in Minnesota.

from

Is Distinguished Philanthropy Still Possible?

Keynote address to the Annual Conference of the Minnesota Council on Foundations, Minneapolis, Minnesota, December 13, 2002.

With the nation and most states in a financial slide, and given the culture and operating styles of most foundations, philanthropy's odds of making a real difference today strike me as being longer than ever. In fact, I have serious doubts whether distinguished philanthropy is still possible.

Yet I have no doubt that we must act as if it is. Our efforts have to be focused, determined and smart. There is much to be done, even if the results turn out a little less distinguished than we'd hoped.

Consider Minnesota—a relatively philanthropy-rich environment, as states go. It has approximately 1,200 foundation and corporate grantmakers, whose assets exceed $12 billion. In the year 2000 they awarded $810 million in charitable grants.[16] That's a very respectable sum. In fact, it has more than doubled since 1993. (This mirrors the national pattern, where grantmaking more than doubled between 1996 and 2000.) In Minnesota, as in the rest of the United States, philanthropy and the nonprofit sector have been fast-growth industries for a decade. But the good times are history.

Put it in perspective. If the same amount of giving in Minnesota two years ago was used to cover the state's current budget deficit, it would fill, maybe, one-fifth of the gap. One-fifth. And that's just the *gap*—not the budget. According to the *Minneapolis Star Tribune*,[17] at least $4 billion needs to be found in the next two and a half years through some mix of expense reduction and revenue enhancement.

This is precisely the time to re-frame what we think and how we operate.

We can argue about the angle of the slide, or the degree of difficulty we are in. But we can't escape the fact that the things we care most about, the economic, civic and ethical health of our people and institutions, are under great and increasing stress. While the economy bumps along, the current and future needs of our fields grow exponentially. Competition for government funding will be increasingly fierce.

But this is precisely the time to re-frame what we think and how we operate. Our first task is to clearly see how this new era has upended us. Then, we can find ways to throw our muscle into the places where philanthropy's very modest power can have its very greatest effect. For let's be clear about our baseline: Foundations are Lilliputians in a world of private-sector and government Gullivers.

But let's not roll over and play dead either. Our power can be used smartly in order to achieve our mission. And yes—we *do* have power.

What Distinguishes Philanthropy

My case is simple: Organized philanthropy plays its game blindfolded and with one arm tied behind its back. We have a large repertoire of unused tools and tactics. We have neglected to create and use our knowledge, our public voice, our financial wealth, our partners and even our high ground. For philanthropy to be distinguished it must unlock and use all these resources.

A first step is to break the false connection many of us make between charity and philanthropy. Many of us act as if they're the same thing. They aren't.

Charity is ancient, honorable and important, but it is not what we do. It's rooted in Judeo-Christian teachings that call for assisting the poor and the weak. Traditionally, it seeks to provide relief. It's largely focused on individuals and deals with symptoms, not causes. Indeed, it is often reactive and as personal for the giver as it is for the recipient.[18]

By contrast, philanthropy is what we do—or should be doing more of. It derives from a

A first step is to break the false connection many of us make between charity and philanthropy.

36

Greco-Roman tradition that speaks more to civic obligation and the needs of the community. It is collective and inevitably political. Philanthropy acts primarily through institutions, not with individuals. And since institutions carry the DNA of our society, that is where deep or large-scale change can happen.

We no longer have the luxury of assuming that small acts of generosity can meet the needs of today—or tomorrow.

Both charity and philanthropy have noble histories. They have secure places in our inventory of human goodness. In fact, the charity–philanthropy–government partnership makes our country unique among nations. It has sparked, fueled and sustained our greatest social movements.

But we no longer have the luxury of assuming that small acts of generosity can meet the needs of today—or tomorrow. The satisfaction we derive from charity seduces us into thinking that, increment by increment, we will have a large impact on our deepest problems. This is false. We must make the distinction: funding soup kitchens (charity) or figuring out why we need soup kitchens in the first place, and then making them unnecessary (philanthropy).

These are the markers of distinguished philanthropy: going after root causes of poverty, inequity and disadvantage, and, by doing so, making lasting institutional and social change.

To be sure, the great majority of funders don't have assets anywhere near those of the great root-cause philanthropists of the last century, the Carnegies and Rosenwalds and Rockefellers. And some are tempted to conclude from that fact that the distinction between charity and philanthropy doesn't apply to them, that tackling root causes demands vast means.

But that's wrong; it does apply. The scale of our current problems just makes the challenge clearer and the search for effective strategies more urgent.

Being small doesn't disqualify us at all. We can take very effective, manageable bites.

Being small doesn't disqualify us at all. We can take very effective, manageable bites. We can work more collaboratively and leverage our dollars. One case in point is the Otto Bremer Foundation's leadership, setting up a collaborative funding pool to build capacity in Hispanic organizations. Another is the St. Paul Foundation's "Diversity Endowment Funds." Joint work, smartly done. That's one step forward.

FIVE STEPS TOWARD EFFECTIVENESS

With the challenge so large, I think we must look inside at our own operating procedures first. We may not be able to balance our states' budgets, but we can do our work much more expertly, and help make the allocations go as far as possible.

Our job has become largely one of due diligence and check-writing. We are more focused on making good grants than on doing distinguished philanthropy. There *is* increased attention being paid to collaboration, building metrics and introducing accountability. But the current paradigm of philanthropy is still discrete, isolated and modest to the point of timidity. Here are five initiatives we can all take to change course and advance our effectiveness:

First, we must become even better listeners and learners. It's hard to look up from our guidelines and time commitments, to take the time to learn from our grantees—to learn what they think as well as what they do. Every observer knows this. One thing I constantly find is grantees feeling put upon, if not abused, by grantmakers. The inherent power imbalance, sometimes made greater by an experience imbalance, hurts relationships and pro- gram implementation. We need to do better, together. (Christine Letts and Bill Ryan of Harvard's Kennedy School have been studying this phenom- enon in an effort to define what makes for "high impact philanthropy."[19])

It's so hard to listen, learn and then *co-create* programs with nonprofit *partners*. Improved com- munication and collaboration need to be a basic job of program staff and presidents. The goal is to be at least as helpful to grantees as grantees are to foundations.

We have to restrain ourselves in initiating our own projects that don't account for the needs or capacity of the field. We need to selectively expand our time and dollar commitments to grantees. Even in this downturn, many foundations probably need to selectively *add* staff.

Second, we must be knowledge-builders and knowledge-sharers. Imagine if funders and grantees made it their point to capture and disseminate all

We have to restrain ourselves in initiating our own projects that don't account for the needs or capacity of the field.

The field has little tradition of collaborative investigation, open communication and broad dissemination.

the useful information they commission, collect or compile. All the due-diligence reports. All the trends in their fields of interest. All the reviews of the local neighborhood leadership. All the GIS maps and capacity analyses of cities and regions. All the evaluations. Reinventing the wheel is costly. Tens of millions of dollars and tens of millions of hours each year can be put to better use.

The fact is, most philanthropy operates in isolation. Knowledge and information are compiled and tucked away. The field itself has little tradition of collaborative investigation, open communication and broad dissemination. That isn't to say fine work isn't produced and dispatched, but that it is neither common nor systemic.

By being knowledge-builders and -sharers we also become connectors of people to information, and enablers of collaboration. We must build hubs of an open network that constantly grows and nurtures its members. This is a key to influence and power.

Third, we must be investors, not just grantmakers. Most of us spend 5 percent of our endowment annually. We treat this IRS rule as the ceiling on what we can give, not the floor. But I would argue that this is small potatoes. For philanthropy to be distinguished, the solution is to be found elsewhere.

We need to think about investing part of our endowments in mission-related ways. There are increasing numbers of examples to show how philanthropy can really walk its talk.

The McCune Charitable Foundation, the largest in New Mexico, has as its mission the revitalization of downtown Albuquerque—and to make significant returns in the process. As part of a joint venture with a private land developer and the city government, the foundation has contributed $5 million in equity and low-interest loans that will start to pay big returns in eight to nine years.

The Libra Foundation of Maine carries 30 percent of its endowment in real estate in and around Portland. It has invested $9 million to revive the Portland Public Market in a blighted neighborhood and is renovating a 1,000-acre parcel containing an abandoned mental hospital to become commercial space and farmland. Libra expects one-third of its grant funds to come from its real estate assets.

For the last five years the small Jacobs Family Foundation (endowment approximately $20 million) has devoted all its funds to one intensely place-based venture in southeast San Diego called Market Creek.[20] Last year the Heron Foundation of New York City decided to use all its endowment, in excess of $300 million, to invest in local communities for financial and social return.

The most substantial and exciting example is the State of California itself. Under its treasurer, Philip Angelides, it has aggressively invested in community development projects, to the tune of more than $475 million. The State's two pension funds have committed 2 percent of their portfolios to

California's underserved communities, including mortgage loans and real estate investments.[21]

Imagine if just 5 percent of the assets of independent foundations went directly into mission-related investing. That would total nearly $25 billion in new, income-earning, recyclable dollars. It equals nearly all the grants made by institutional philanthropy in the year 2000. The opportunities are solid, numerous and growing, and there are enough intermediaries around to help foundations willing to make the investment. Double the size of our investment in the sector? Absolutely.

Fourth, we must be resolute advocates in the service of our mission. The task is both national and local, and the two are often intertwined.

For example, why not consider voting our proxies when corporate behavior is objectionable? The country's largest public pension fund, CalPERS, has taken this step. It voted last month to "ask three major corporations to become American companies again," giving up the offshore addresses that permit them to escape taxes and reduce shareholders' rights.[22] Or, why shouldn't foundations comment (as is their right) on the Securities and Exchange Commission's proposed rules to have mutual funds publicly reveal how they vote on corporate issues?

Why should we do this? Not because we are anti-corporate, but because as the corporate tax base shrinks, or flees into offshore tax havens, the burden of paying for economic and social programs shifts to individuals, or just disappears.

Also, corporations are part of the American compact. They are stakeholders, just as we are stockholders. And we all have a direct responsibility to sustain the common good. Less money for important programs hurts us all and brings less fairness in the tax system. When collections are down, services are cut, real people suffer—and nonprofits usually get left holding the bag.

Advocacy is educational, absolutely legal and often necessary. Foundations simply have to find their public voice, and not just occasionally fund others to do it. When we do, we will have a far greater impact on the issues we care deeply about. Effective advocacy is part of our job—and we cannot have lasting impact without it.

Finally, we must be capacity-builders. I say this because so much of our funding focuses on programs and planning. Most foundations give short shrift to nonprofit infrastructure. They don't watch to ensure that staff will be capable of delivering on their promises. They pay little heed to reasonable indirect costs.

The best example of systematic capacity-building I know has been developed by the Edna McConnell Clark Foundation in New York City. The foundation has chosen to strengthen a small number of youth-serving organizations for the long term. It has committed $25 million annually to nonprofits who build detailed business plans and

As the corporate tax base shrinks, the burden of paying for economic and social programs shifts to individuals, or just disappears.

Philanthropy can
actively invest
in its mission.
It can advocate
and help others
advocate, too.

do ongoing monitoring, which the foundation and the organization do together. Several million dollars are slated to go to each grantee to keep it sturdy, competent and at the top of its class in service delivery.[23]

Another similar example is found in the Washington, D.C., region by Venture Philanthropy Partners. VPP is taking up the role of investor, participant, technical assistance provider, mentor, advocate and funder of the groups it has identified.

Our toolbox must include institution-building, at *both* foundations and nonprofits, since both are key to getting at root-cause problems.

LISTENERS, INVESTORS, COLLABORATORS

What all this adds up to is a model of foundations doing distinguished philanthropy in good times and in bad. It calls for a philanthropy that actively listens, learns, helps, partners, networks, develops and transmits knowledge to its colleagues and its nonprofit partners. It connects them to each other and enables them to build skills and work together for greater impact.

It says that philanthropy can actively *invest* in its mission. It can advocate and help others advocate, too, in a constantly growing, interactive network of genuine allies. It says our collective power is greater than our grant money. Power comes from our capacity to analyze and share data, develop positions, collaborate on policy as well as programs, teach others and ourselves, and course-correct to do better the next time.

If we do this, we will attack our root-cause problems together and make much headway in solving them—despite the financial slide and perilous times. Ultimately, by heading into the fray together, with our talents, fortunes and voices, we can approach the standards of distinction our philanthropic ancestors set down for us.

For its 2006 annual conference, the Center for Effective Philanthropy put down a hard challenge: to describe barriers to improved foundation performance and to offer pointers toward a more effective philanthropy. These comments sum up my attempt at an answer.

References to federal fiscal policy and the budget deficit midway through this discussion are based on circumstances in 2005 and 2006, when the Treasury Department's audited financial statement showed a deficit of $760 billion for FY 2005. The figure rose to $3.5 trillion when Social Security and Medicare were included.

from

Doing Better — It Isn't About the Money

Speech to the Fifth Annual Conference of the Center for Effective Philanthropy, New York City, New York, September 14, 2006.

However much good foundations do, and we do a lot of it, we all operate in a world of unlimited choice in the programs we fund and the approaches we take. Some are smart, some are dopey. Some are transparent, some are foggy. Some are strategic, some are haphazard. The latitude we enjoy is heightened by the fact that we also are free from public scrutiny. There are no shareholders, no ratings agencies, no oversight authorities, no voters or grantees on our backs. No other institutions, I think, have such a limitless field of play.

Except for the most flagrant law-breaking, there also are no performance standards. So we tend to be all-over-the-map in every conceivable program area, in strategic approaches and on field-wide subjects ranging from the role of advocacy to the cost of payout.

Yet we all feel limited. We sense a universe of constraints barring our way to real effectiveness and lasting achievement. Ask why foundations don't accomplish more, perform better, advance farther, and you'll get a catalogue of barriers from nearly every knowledgeable player and observer. Yet the obvious, paradoxical question is: *How can there be so many barriers to performance when there are so few boundaries to hem us in?*

The core of the answer, I think, is this: The biggest barrier to improved foundation perform-ance is our own constraining "mental model" about how we should conduct ourselves. It's not just what we do; it's our perception of the world and how we think. Our constraints don't come from the outside world; they come from within. If we can overcome this, our effectiveness will surely rise.

By "mental models" I mean "deeply held internal images of how the world works, images that limit us to familiar ways of thinking and acting."[24] Our mental models are outmoded and have remained so for decades. There are three reasons for this.

First, as a community we don't engage much in *self-reflection*—even though we often say we wish

> The biggest barrier to improved foundation performance is our own constraining 'mental model.'

we had the time to do it. Taking the time to deepen our knowledge of the external environment, the trends and stresses in our field, and especially our own experiences, is critical to improving performance. Of course, our grantees have even less time to reflect than we do. Absent self-reflection, improved performance may well be accidental, or hard to systematize and harder to build upon.

Since we operate in a world without standards, there is virtually no *critical analysis* of performance.

Second, since we operate in a world without standards, there is virtually no *critical analysis* of performance. Outsiders don't write much about us. Bad press usually focuses on hubris and bizarre personal behavior. In those rare cases of "real" public criticism, our mores suggest we have little responsibility to publicly respond, to defend, to argue, to grapple, to enlighten. Things tend to go silent.

Like everyone, we're reluctant to hold up a mirror to ourselves. The last serious "insider" account of specific foundations and their weaknesses was Waldemar Nielsen's *The Golden Donors*.[25] It was published 21 years ago, and for the rest of his life Nielsen became a slightly tainted, faintly "dissed" colleague.

But we have also let pass efforts to recognize and reward high-quality accomplishment in a way that colleagues feel compelled to adapt. In short, neither good practice nor bad practice causes us to respond.

Third, systematic, ongoing *data collection and dissemination* hasn't evolved to a standard practice in our field—even when this information would help us to learn and improve our performance. We like to think we are what Paul Ylvisaker called "society's passing gear," but we have little hard evidence to back up such a claim.

In the past five years the Center for Effective Philanthropy has begun to systematically improve upon this data drought, and the results have been notable. Thanks to them we know a lot more about who we are, how we act and how we are perceived by our grantees. It's also an encouraging sign that funders are willing to pay for CEP's expertise.

68,000 'PARALLEL PLAYERS'

A lot of foundations look remarkably like sovereign nation–states of the 19th and 20th centuries, accountable only to themselves. For a sovereign, there is no compelling need to reflect, respond to criticism, share information...to be accountable. There aren't any consequences for not doing so. Neither are there incentives to improve. Only in those rare moments when a restive Congress focuses on our policies or our perquisites do we see that some institutions are more sovereign, and more powerful, than others. The good news is that we have begun to take accountability seriously— as it relates to our own internal practices, and certainly to those of our grantees.

Do foundations really want hard data? Do we really value critical analysis and reflection? Do we fully

Do foundations really want hard data? Do we fully understand the strategic importance of what we know?

49

understand the strategic importance of sharing what we know and what we do? History would probably answer "no."

One indicator is that foundations do very little to support and sustain the core research organizations of our own sector—the ones we almost derisively call "infrastructure" groups. The field doesn't seem to want sectoral data and, without much funding, supply is low. This depresses demand further.

There's one especially important result of this sovereignty model. It's our inability to see that 68,000 American foundations are one interlocking system, part of a dynamic whole. We often act only as individual players without any inherent connection to our colleagues. Since we don't see this connection, we find it unnecessary to work together, marshal our individual strengths and have a much greater collective impact on the way the system works for us and our grantees. In times like these, such behavior amounts to shooting ourselves in both feet.

Here's the truth: The Center for Effective Philanthropy, in research over the last five years, has found a variety of cases of foundations with *no* awareness of other funders working in the same grantmaking field, often in the same geographic area. What CEP has confirmed is case after case of "parallel play" in philanthropy.

We often act only as individual players without any inherent connection to our colleagues.

Now, would knowing how well we are doing individually help us to get a better handle on the equally important question: How is philanthropy-as-a-whole doing? Is our mutual desire to build a society that is fairer, more equitable and richer in opportunity getting closer or slipping away?

In sum, the barriers we've built create two interrelated issues. The first is how to raise our effectiveness foundation by foundation. The second is how to work more effectively together to create broad social change.

On the first issue, there is some reason for optimism. In the past few years, some foundations have begun to engage in serious reflection about their work, and what real progress really takes. The Surdna Foundation is moving in this direction. Like several others, we're intentionally, openly talking—board and staff together—about impact and effectiveness, about how to get there and how to understand progress. We're unpacking our assumptions and our "theories of change." We're asking ourselves some tough questions about our goals and strategies, what we can realistically accomplish with our limited resources, how the size, number and duration of grants relates to feasibility, and how we can better collaborate with others to meet our goals. We have also increasingly moved to buckle programs in two or three areas to give us more bang for the buck (for instance, we're aligning our community development and environment programs).

To a large degree, these are questions we have long been asking our grantees. Effective performance, staffing, linking goals to resources and resources

The barriers we've built create two interrelated issues: how to raise our effectiveness foundation by foundation, and how to work more effectively together.

No matter how well individual foundations perform, the results of a single funder have too little lift to move huge social systems.

to programs. Board capacity. Collaboration and communication. It's not that hard to turn these questions back on ourselves to answer as well.

As more foundations move down this road, we can expect our impact to be greater. Our strategies for how we implement our goals are bound to get sharper and smarter. At long last, we may get to the place where we can not only define impact, but also know how and why progress has happened.

On the second issue—effectiveness on a collective, systems level—I am not hopeful. Little has changed since I entered philanthropy 17 years ago. Working together is still a sometime thing, despite the fact that our strength to affect the issues we work on depends totally on linking arms and leveraging our power together. Even Bill and Melinda Gates, with resources several times the size of the next-largest foundation, readily acknowledge this. No matter how well individual foundations perform, the results of a single funder have too little lift to move huge social systems like education, health care and the environment. Sovereignty, sad to say, is still king.

What is clear to me is how urgent such collaboration is. It's a foregone conclusion that, in the program areas we're interested in, we're being pounded. Funding from Washington is in sharp decline, and that shrinkage threatens not only our mission, but the very people we serve.[26, 27]

Reports by the Center on Budget and Policy

Priorities make the point again and again: The discretionary federal budget is being slashed to pay for our huge budget deficit. Tax cuts for the richest 1 percent are permitting two economies and two societies to take root. We're borrowing heavily against our future. And it will get worse. If tax cuts are extended, which is likely, new Senate budget rules would trigger automatic, additional cuts on top of the deep discretionary cuts called for. Entitlement programs like Medicare and Medicaid would be increasingly threatened, then probably reduced, and reduced again and again. Discretionary programs in, say, affordable housing, education, food stamps and public health could gradually disappear.

Foundations do have a choice. We can continue under the old sovereignty mindset and become increasingly irrelevant, no matter how well we are run. In this case, dollars will be stretched further, programs gradually marginalized, impact systematically reduced, and communities increasingly stressed out and vulnerable.

Or we can decide to come together around program themes, design projects that focus on changing public policy, build alliances with colleagues (including grantees), speak out, advocate and help shift the credo of Social Darwinism now promoted by the federal government. This won't happen until we see that it is in our collective interest to work to uphold America's social compact.

We can decide to come together around program themes, speak out, advocate and help shift the credo of Social Darwinism.

START FROM THE TOP: BOARDS OF DIRECTORS

There is no single answer to improving internal effectiveness and building strong operating coalitions. But there is one institution that can play a vital role in both. That is the board of directors. My view is that we need to re-think how boards are constituted and how they work. I say this knowing that the re-thinking of board composition, role and process is making a positive difference at Surdna, where the relationship between board and staff has grown increasingly productive and harmonious over the years.

What do boards really do? There's general agreement that their core functions are to assure fiscal honesty, hire and fire the CEO, and make major strategic decisions for staff to implement. That's the mental model.

In actual fact, good accountants can assure fiscal honesty. In truth, they are the people who uncover these problems anyway. Boards do hire and fire CEOs, yet their sub-par appointments are as common as their great choices. And boards' strategic decisions largely fall into two camps: They ratify the directions the staff proposes, or they go their own way and focus on parochial or personal interests.

It's the rare board that exceeds this modest standard. It's the rare board that really offers true, informed, constant value to the CEO, the foundation and the field.

Most often, little is really asked of boards, and little is given. Why is this? In creating their boards, foundations have the opportunity to build a brains trust, a shaper of effective programs, as well as their advocate, and a representative in the larger world. Shouldn't we adjust our old model and bring it into the 21st century?

I think the answer is "yes," so here are some important questions that follow from that premise:

In creating their boards, foundations have the opportunity to build a brains trust.

- Should there be written criteria for board membership and written job descriptions of what is A+ service?

- Should boards be deliberately chosen to enhance program quality, to bring other perspectives and skills directly to the task?

- Should boards reflect a diversity of opinions, color and class, particularly when their organization's programs involve such diversity?

- Should boards be strong public advocates when their involvement would build civic consciousness or move the legislative process?

- Should boards be active in using their networks and contacts to stimulate funder coalitions?

- Should boards grade their performance on a regular basis and report back to their stakeholders and staff on the results?

- Should board members resign if their performance is found to be sub-standard?

All these questions make sense. And CEOs (and senior staff) are the ones who will have to raise them with our boards. Who else will?

It's the CEO's task to be proactive and to create high standards of performance for staffs and boards. CEOs are the drivers of improvement, internal and external. They are the ones who uphold their foundations' missions every working day.

Think about what boards and staffs could be if entropy didn't set in.

My questions are also researchable. It would be helpful to gather data and analyze boards and their possibilities. That critical analysis could be the beginning of clearer standards and better governance models.

Boards need not be among the field's barriers to sustained high performance. Quite the opposite, they can help assure it. Unexamined, like all institutions, they will fall to their lowest common denominator. But think about what boards and staffs could be if entropy didn't set in. Think about what philanthropy could be if foundations not only improved their individual performance, but linked up and maximized their strength to build a better world.

So this is my case, and it's really quite simple: We can choose to be the solution if we decide, as the great American philosopher Emeril Lagasse says, to "kick it up a notch." We have it within our power to make a much bigger impact on the inequity and scarcity that holds our society back. We don't have to finish the job, but we have to start it—and very, very soon.

FOOTNOTES FOR FROM PURPOSE TO POWER

[1] Waldemar A. Nielsen, *Inside American Philanthropy: The Dramas of Donorship*, University of Oklahoma Press, 1996, pp. 41, 44.

[2] Michael A. Fletcher, "Big Gift to Schools Brings Small Gains," *Washington Post*, June 12, 2002, p. A02.

[3] Paul Ylvisaker, "The Relationship Between Private Philanthropy and Government," in *Conscience and Community: The Legacy of Paul Ylvisaker*, edited by Virginia M. Esposito, New York: Peter Lang Publishing, 1999, p. 310.

[4] *New York Times*, April 25, 2002, p. A20 and *Chicago Tribune*, April 25, 2002, Metro p. 1.

[5] Paul Ylvisaker, "The Spirit of Philanthropy and the Soul of Those Who Manage It," in *Conscience and Community*, p. 346.

[6] System: "An interrelated complex of elements that is coherently organized around some function or purpose. A system is more than the sum of its parts. It can exhibit self-preserving, adaptive, dynamic, goal-seeking and/or evolutionary behavior." From "Systemability: A workbook on Systems Thinking, Sustainability, and Funding," unpublished notes from a two-day workshop January 12–13, 2001 prepared by the Sustainability Institute. A fine introduction to systems thinking is found in Peter Senge, et al., *The Fifth Discipline Fieldbook*, New York: Doubleday, 1994, pp. 87–190.

[7] Daniel Ben-Horin, President, Compumentor, e-mail January 26, 2001.

[8] "Strategic Positioning and the Financing of Nonprofit Organizations," Working Paper #2 in the Hauser Center's series, Harvard University, 2000.

[9] See especially *Social Purpose Enterprises and Venture Philanthropy in the New Millennium*, Jed Emerson, 3 volumes, San Francisco: The Roberts Enterprise Development Fund, 1999.

[10] *Bowling Alone: The Collapse and Revival of American Community*, Robert D. Putnam, New York: Simon and Schuster, 2000, p. 19.

[11] "On Schools as Learning Organizations: A Conversation with Peter Senge," John O'Neil, *Educational Leadership*, April 1995, p. 22

[12] A notable case of mapping is done annually by the Sierra Business Council. Some cities, like Jacksonville, Florida, have also perfected the mapping approach.

[13] "The Value Creation Dilemma: New Building Blocks for the Experience Revolution," C. K. Prahalad and Venkatram Ramaswamy, July 30, 2001, unpublished.

[14] Ibid. p. 27.

[15] Ibid. p. 29.

[16] "Minnesota Grantmaking 2003 Outlook Report," Minnesota Council on Foundations, December 2002.

[17] "State Budget Deficit to Top $4.5 Billion," December 4, 2002.

[18] For parts of this discussion, see Paul Ylvisaker's speech "The Spirit of Philanthropy" in *Conscience and Community*, pp. 340–347; Barry D. Karl and Stanley N. Katz, "Foundations and Ruling Class Elites," *Daedalus*, Winter 1987, vol. 116, no. 1; and Vartan Gregorian, "President's Essay," *Carnegie Corporation 2000 Annual Report*, Carnegie Corporation of New York, Website: www.carnegie.org.

[19] See Letts, Christine W. and Ryan, William P., draft working paper "High Engagement Philanthropy: Filling the Performance Gap," July 23, 2002.

[20] For several additional examples, see "Doing Well By Doing Good: Innovative Foundation Investments in Place-Based Smart Growth Development," a report by the Funders' Network for Smart Growth and Livable Communities, September 2002.

[21] Remarks by Phil Angelides, Treasurer, State of California, at the Rainbow / PUSH Digital Solutions Conference, San Jose, California, April 25, 2002.

[22] *New York Times*, November 17 and 19, 2002.

[23] "EMCF: A New Approach to an Old Foundation," Harvard Business School Case Study, Allen Grossman and Daniel Curran, 2002.

[24] Peter M. Senge, *The Fifth Discipline*, Doubleday, 1990, p. 174, italics added.

[25] Waldemar A. Nielsen, *The Golden Donors*, E.P. Dutton, New York, 1985.

[26] James Horney, "New CBO Deficit Estimates That Without the Tax Cuts, the Budget Would be Balanced," Center for Budget and Policy Priorities, August 8, 2006.

[27] Robert Greenstein, "Combined Effect of Senate Proposals Would Be to Finance Near-Repeal of the Estate Tax with Cuts in Medicare, Veterans Benefits, School Lunches and Other Programs," Center for Budget and Policy Priorities, August 9, 2006.

2

Higher Values, Bottom Lines

THE FUTURE OF THE NONPROFIT SECTOR
IN THE AGE OF ENTERPRISE

The idea that some nonprofits can, or should, pursue earned revenue and run profitable businesses draws a lot of hyperbole, both positive and negative. It is an idea with which I have a long personal history, and no doubt a few hyperboles of my own to offer. But by the time I gave this talk, in mid-2005, my own history as a nonprofit entrepreneur was well in the past. Instead, at that point, I found myself in a role I had never really thought likely: that of an elder statesman in a still-inchoate but growing field—one with a national membership, a seminal body of scholarship focused on its activities, and a healthy cadre of vocal critics.

Few of us who grappled with this heterodox idea a couple of decades ago had much reason to worry that our ideas would someday raise important questions for the American nonprofit sector. We were usually happy when our work drew any interest at all. Now, though, the issue of social enterprise does, at least occasionally, raise some provocative and far-reaching questions. Though it's too soon to offer conclusive answers, I try to grapple here with some of the issues facing the field, and the sector, as the idea of nonprofit entrepreneurship enters its second quarter-century.

from

Twenty-Five Years of Social Entrepreneurship in Twenty-Five Minutes

Comments upon receiving the first Social Enterprise Award for Leadership in Financing from the Social Enterprise Alliance at its Annual Conference, Milwaukee, Wisconsin, April 19, 2005.

In recent years, national enthusiasm has waxed and waned, and waxed again, over the prospect of public-interest organizations earning revenue by running businesses. While no one claims this approach is any kind of panacea—or, at least, no one with any credibility—the idea has a kind of automatic appeal. It has even, in some circles, acquired something of a cult following. As with so much else in the 21st-century nonprofit sector, there is enormous opportunity in this entrepreneurship idea, and equally great risk, too. Fortunately, the discussion about both has been a lively and promising one.

I arrive at this viewpoint with some firsthand experience to back it up. I started the first organization devoted to helping nonprofits earn money as well as beg for it. It was 1980. With a small grant from the Rockefeller Brothers Fund, I sought— without really knowing it—to break new ground in the nonprofit sector. I had no idea how parched and hard that ground was.

So, in typical entrepreneur's fashion, I sublet some space next to the copy machine from another nonprofit, had business cards made up and applied for 501(c)(3) status. Then I set about promoting the idea that, for nonprofits, earning money was as plausible as getting grants—though very different, too. The organization was called New Ventures.

The resistance to this concept was amazing. For some it was the "nuclear option." People objected on moral grounds, on ethical grounds, on legal grounds, on business grounds, on technical grounds and, when all else failed, on personal grounds. As I said, the ground was very hard.

Only in 1983 did the *Harvard Business Review* publish the first article (mine) on nonprofit venturing, titled "Should Not-For-Profits Go Into Business?" In fact, according to G. G. Michelson,

There is enormous opportunity in this entrepreneurship idea, and equally great risk, too.

who was then a member of the *HBR* board, it was the first article the journal had *ever* printed dealing with the nonprofit sector.

Now, I waited for vindication, which didn't come. I spoke at the Council of Foundations and Independent Sector and waited for a surge of grants, which didn't come either. I started to create and edit a book. I gave workshops on nonprofit venturing around the country, thinking they would be my loss leader. In fact, there were too many loss leaders to count. All lost; hardly any led.

And then came my first big break.

(First, though, a brief aside: At least two decades had passed before I told this story publicly. I'm certain there are specifics I've long forgotten, or which I have somewhat askew. I did review the story with David Andrews, who was then the project director at Planned Parenthood Federation of America and a key actor in this story, and he confirms its accuracy. When I finally told the story, I offered an actual artifact as evidence: a strip of six condoms, with the Planned Parenthood logo attractively stamped on each wrapper. I passed them around the room to give people a good look. I didn't really mind if the package didn't make its way back to the podium. But given that this was an old story even then, I guess the audience had a reasonable grasp of the concept of "shelf life." I have that strip of condoms to this day.)

The 'Social Entrepreneur's Rush'

I was sitting in my little office in the early 1980s when the phone rang. I answered it to hear the voice of a senior employee of Planned Parenthood. He told me PPFA had ordered and purchased an enormous quantity of high-quality, lubricated condoms (say, a hundred thousand dozen or some such figure) from a vendor in Taiwan, and they were about to land on the docks of Bayonne, New Jersey, in just a few days. PPFA's intention was to sell the strips of six condoms in its clinics and offices around the country to clients and thus (a) contribute to the fulfillment of its mission, (b) educate all who used or inquired about its services, and (c) earn income to help the organization expand its work.

Problem was, they had no real idea how to run this enterprise. They had no business plan to speak of, and they wanted to get the program running ASAP. Could New Ventures help?

Could we help? *Could we help?* Does it rain in Spain? We agreed to meet soon after the call to discuss the situation.

Now, I have to tell you, this is a pure case of what I call "the social entrepreneur's rush." At a moment like this it suddenly hits you that you not only have a potentially gargantuan financial winner, but you also have the hook into making real social change. You don't get many moments like that, but when it happens, the thrill of discovery

A potentially gargantuan financial winner, with a hook into making real social change.

is fairly dizzying. With the rush come the fantasies. Why stop with condoms? After condoms there are foams. Then jellies. Then diapers! Then healthy baby foods! Then a *Fortune 500 nonprofit*!

Then, if you have your wits about you, you breathe deeply, compartmentalize the golden opportunity, and get to work.

New Ventures took on the task of drafting a business and marketing plan to help PPFA move the project to full execution. In essence, it was decided to distribute the condoms to all clinics and offices where they would be sold at a certain price with respectable margins. Staff of the clinics would act as educators and salespeople, and the product would be placed prominently, with relevant written material, so that visitors could see it and buy it.

But then another scenario heaved into view. Senior staff at the national office of PPFA, no less enthusiastic than I was, saw the obvious opportunity to brand and sell the condoms to a mass retail market—in nothing less than national, chain drug stores. They'd be prominently displayed behind the pharmacy cash register (where such items are always found). But to roll this out successfully, they'd need a corporate partner of enormous clout to demand and get shelf space and the best possible placement. Now we could *really* imagine breathtaking profits. Planned Parenthood could make a giant leap in the long march toward large market share and a powerful household name. National staff at PPFA instantly grasped the scale of the opportunity and went looking for a private sector partner, eventually landing on American Home Products. AHP was one of the largest companies in the retail drug market-place with enormous clout in pharmacies. (AHP, for various unrelated reasons, went belly up several years ago. Planned Parenthood is still here.)

As AHP stepped in, New Ventures' role gradually diminished. It became a matter of contracts and licensing and percentages and negotiations among dozens of lawyers representing I-don't-know-how-many parties. Still, even in a peripheral role, it was tremendously exciting to be part of these meetings, slowly working toward, if I may say, the consummation of a grand business romance. Of course, AHP would have to be in the driver's seat now, controlling virtually all product marketing, sales, inventories, promotions, advertising and all the rest.

And then, as they say, it all hit the fan. Conflict flared up over AHP's natural desire to move quickly and far into other lines of contraceptive-related products. After all, AHP's job was to move product —which, obviously, is how you make profits. This commercial approach triggered considerable fear in the ranks of numerous large PPFA affiliates, who had a twofold, if contradictory, stance regarding the enterprise. First, they saw it as a case of selling out to corporate interests that had different purposes from those of PPFA. Some were additionally nervous about what they saw as an improper use of the

This commercial approach triggered considerable fear.

nonprofit's service mark.

Second, they didn't want the national office to run the project anyway. So, while they opposed the venture, they also demanded that the affiliates get most of the profits from condom sales. Finally, extensive product testing and the cost of extra insurance coverage from Lloyd's of London (PPFA was extremely liability-conscious) threatened to erode profit margins. Positions of PPFA and AHP executives began to harden, as did the respective positions of PPFA-national and its key affiliates. Negotiations got harder. Then they floundered. Then the project died.

A billion-dollar social enterprise, up in smoke. Or at least that's how it felt.

Planned Parenthood and its chapters ultimately reverted to their own cultural standard. The organization distributed the condoms throughout its network, where they were frequently put in large fish bowls in the waiting rooms with a sign that read "Please Take." People took. Over time, they were all given away. The stevedores of Bayonne never lifted another Planned Parenthood condom again.

As I'll note in a minute, despite the time, money and risk the national office took to make this enterprise work, it ultimately confronted too many antagonists to succeed. The project became an organizational nightmare, and it scared many in the organization who were decidedly more skeptical and less entrepreneurial. The resistance just became

A billion-dollar social enterprise, up in smoke.

too great to continue. In turn, I'm sure I fell into what might be called "social entrepreneur's depression," which, being the serial problem-solvers that we are, probably lasted only a few weeks—till a new world-beater project heaved into my imagination.

From Struggling Startup to Struggling Field

So what were the lessons that carry over till today?

First, that any enterprise is tough to do, and that nonprofit enterprise is almost certainly tougher, especially if taken to scale. It's not the first sale that's important, it's the second, third and fourth. At any time, and in a dozen ways, the rug can be pulled from under you. Most practitioners know that, or they learn it very quickly.

Second, it's never easy to partner with the private sector, especially an aggressive company that believes it must have tremendous control in order to succeed in the marketplace. Conflict over control squeezed much of the life out of the project. But it also threw into bold relief a third issue: cultural differences within (and without) the organization. Over and over, "moral" issues of mission vs. money, of "selling out," arose. Without unanimity on the most basic values, the foundation on which to build a business will always be insecure.

Finally, you have to know when to hold 'em and when to fold 'em. Many practitioners may know that, but many don't. And many funders don't

Over and over, 'moral' issues of mission vs. money, of 'selling out' arose.

69

know it, either.

I folded New Ventures in 1989 after nine exciting and exhausting years. I loved what I did. I got off on being a flashing star in a dark universe. New Ventures had grown to seven full-time employees and earned about half its money. And that was critically important to us. After all, if we couldn't earn our money, the hybrid business model we were trying to establish would have tanked—and poisoned the concept for years to come. The idea didn't die. On the contrary, it has grown dramatically.

Still, we couldn't afford a good benefits package, contracts were always erratic, and nonprofits didn't pay much or on time. Foundation support was starting to wane. Marketing to both funders and clients never got easier; in a real sense, we never turned the proverbial corner.

The day I turned off the lights and tore up my business cards, I had no idea that this concept and little venture could actually become a *field*! Yet, look at it now and how it's developing. It has become such a hot ticket that, in 2005, we got another article in the *Harvard Business Review*—but this time, it was a salutary cooling-off notice by Jeff Bradach and William Foster, putting up all the warning signs.[1] The article is an excellent reminder of the difficulties of mixing nonprofit and for-profit approaches and the mythology of success.

And there's been pushback, too, including responses to the *HBR* article by Billy Shore and, in

The Nation, by Michael Shuman and Merrian Fuller.[2]
Both were much more positive about social venturing. Now we have an explosion of talk and
writing about social enterprise. We've got the Skoll
Social Entrepreneurship awards, the Pew/Goldman
Sachs international competition, the *Fast Company*
"top ten," the "blended value" theory, the Omidyar
initiatives, New Profit and the Social Enterprise
Alliance.

Now we have an explosion of talk and writing about social enterprise.

Even President Bush has taken notice. In a cer-
emony at the White House in early 2005, he asked,
"Are we encouraging social enterprise in America?
That's one of my favorite words…"[3]

Social entrepreneurship may not yet be a "field,"
but it has stoked a deep human interest in creating
an authentic "double bottom line."

Still, the President's comments and all the other
expressions of ebullience don't change the real world;
more likely, they confuse it. Not only are all the old
issues still with us—culture, money, organization,
management, leadership, markets—there are newer
ones too: state and local cutbacks, increasingly fragile
social service delivery systems, and an increased
suspicion of nonprofits, which has moved into high
gear. We have our work cut out for us.

FRANKNESS, FRIENDS AND FUNDERS

In that vein, let me offer four suggestions for going
forward that might increase the chances that social
entrepreneurship will survive—and even grow:

First, we need to dampen the puffery and exaggeration about social enterprise and nonprofit venturing. Not the enthusiasm, just the yak-yak that makes us even more vulnerable to criticism, misunderstanding and failure. Nothing will drag us down like hype and hypocrisy. The more claims are made for social enterprise, and the more kinds of activity get wrapped in its mantle, the closer it comes to losing its meaning. Practitioners and funders alike can sharpen the meaning of what it is we stand for and what we do. I think we are on the road here.

> The more claims are made for social enterprise, the closer it comes to losing its meaning.

Simultaneously, practicing or aspiring social entrepreneurs need to look hard for "first cousins" with whom they can share experiences and projects. I'm thinking of organizations like the Community Development Venture Capital Association, or social investment funds (itself a slippery term), community loan pools, and users of the New Markets Tax Credits. Create joint ventures. Build alliances across boundaries. And, above all, *make what you do as open-source as possible*. Here, there's lots of opportunity to experiment.

Third (as if I had to say this), don't expect foundations to deliver. Often, we funders dribble some planning money down the chest of social enterprises and then leave them to clean themselves up. Or we work on our own timetables, with little regard for the marketplace. I've always believed that when it comes to philanthropic equity investments and debt, a fast "no" is worth more than a near-endless "maybe."

The principle for anyone seeking philanthropic investors is: Talk back to funders when you think you're right. You are their deal flow. And find a few staunch allies, as I did, to make your toehold into a solid place to stand.

Finally, we should try, together, to work through the toughest question of all: *How much time do you want to spend building your enterprise, and how much time can you spend on building the field of social entrepreneurship?* It's hard enough to do one of them, but both are essential.

Entrepreneurs are single-minded, persevering and optimistic. They are also notorious non-sharers. But share they must. It's urgent that the best enterprises succeed. But it's also urgent that their creators not exist in an isolated, poorly understood, stressed-out environment. So they need to build a "field" as much for their own sake as for the greater good. Build a space that willingly shares its winning ideas. Help others find sources of money. Tell unvarnished stories of success and failure. You see, "worst practice" usually is a better teacher than "best practice."

Doing all this demands candor, truth-telling and commitment to collective success. This is the big, exciting, daunting challenge today. Honestly, I don't know how to do it. I think it's the next big task for the emerging field, its coalescing organizations

'Worst practice' is usually a better teacher than 'best practice.'

73

and its individual members.

Twenty-five years ago it was impossible to even conceive of this opportunity. But now we're on the threshold. Let's go to it!

The first version
of this talk, with
a different title,
was delivered
to the Council on
Foundations' annual
conference in New
Orleans, April 1999.
This text combines
elements of both the
Aspen and the New
Orleans versions.
Although my
approach in this case
draws most of its
examples from the
field of human
services and welfare
reform, the argument
applies with only
minor variation to
much of the rest of
the nonprofit sector.
    A lot has changed
since I first wrote
this speech, yet as I
revise my text nearly
eight years later,
I don't find much
reason to alter what
I said back then.
The problems of
delivering services
to the poor, like the
poor themselves
(as the phrase goes),
will always be with
us. The problems
may just present
themselves differently.
That noted, I have
updated some of
the text toward the
end of this speech
to account for the
twists and turns of
more recent years.

from

The Nonprofit Sector and the Market: Challenges and Opportunities

Like most of us, as the great jurist Oliver Wendell Holmes got older, he got progressively more absent-minded. Once, on a train trip to Washington, D.C., he was asked for his ticket, but could not locate it. He searched his pockets, his briefcase and his seat. No luck. He became increasingly distraught.

The conductor, knowing Mr. Holmes and his reputation, said reassuringly: "Never mind, sir. When

*Remarks at the Aspen
Institute Nonprofit
Sector Strategy Group,
Aspen, Colorado,
August 14, 1999.*

you find it, I'm sure you will mail it in." But this wasn't any comfort at all. "Mr. Conductor," Justice Holmes replied, "you don't understand. The question is not 'Where is my ticket?' The question is, 'Where am I going?'"[4]

At this moment, nonprofits throughout the country—particularly those providing human services—are asking precisely the same question. They have every right to be as disoriented as Justice Holmes. So do we.

The confusion can be directly attributed to the public sector's growing love affair with privatization and competition. This is changing the service delivery landscape profoundly.

For one thing, governments on all levels are increasingly turning to an attractive new friend, private enterprise, to help them carry out their responsibilities. They are contracting out these obligations by competitive bid.

For another, the new rules of the marketplace are fracturing the old relationship between government and its service providers.

In order to adapt to these new realities, human service organizations are going in three different directions: Some mimic the private sector. Others try to ignore the market. Most are seeking an ill-defined, pragmatic middle ground. They try to adhere to their traditional charitable principles, maintain partial independence and improve their management capacity—all at the same time.

The new rules of the marketplace are fracturing the old relationship between government and its service providers.

To find the right strategy will require going beyond those familiar archetypes that frame our knowledge. You know, government regulates and defends us; the private sector provides goods and services for us; and nonprofits foster the civic and charitable spirit in us. These are all true, but they're much too one-dimensional.

We need to recognize and understand that each sector also acts and reacts to the work and the behavior of the others. Together, they provide a foundation for our unique American culture. They are a three-legged stool. If you shorten one leg, the stool will wobble. If you shorten it too much, the stool will fall.

BIDDING AGAINST GOLIATH

Today, many people in high places in government and business believe fervently that privatization will cure whatever ails us—and will do it at a substantially reduced cost. The public and the news media are equally enthusiastic. They have embraced a very compelling idea: social progress at wholesale prices. What a deal!

But is it a *good* deal? Are we going in the right direction? I believe we are in the early stages of a radical restructuring of service delivery. Authority and responsibility are shifting quickly. Prudence demands we look at what is happening dispassionately. Then we can determine what to do to preserve our integrity, our values and our

Social progress at wholesale prices. What a deal!

commitment to the disadvantaged.

Some history: Since the beginning of the Great Society in the mid-1960s, nonprofits have contracted with government to deliver services. These organizations developed invaluable knowledge and skills. They acquired unique insight into this country's most serious social and economic problems.

Small-scale or neighborhood-based groups were the most common delivery mechanism. The work was decentralized, mission-driven and insulated from serious competition.

In general, the private sector stayed away from the human side of human services. It saw little chance for profit and abundant management headaches. Then in 1996 *everything changed*. The cause was the passage of welfare reform legislation, which broke the nonprofit–government lock on service delivery. The $250 billion welfare machine now looked like a ripe business opportunity.

Formally known as the Personal Responsibility and Work Opportunity Reconciliation Act of 1996, the law essentially certified the outright failure of what the welfare system had by then become. Its most dramatic provisions were a five-year lifetime limit on public assistance and a two-year deadline for most welfare recipients to get employment. And they *had* to get employment.

Implementation was "devolved" to the states. Dollars were channeled through flexible block grants. Because the funding formulas were based

The $250 billion welfare machine now looked like a ripe business opportunity.

on caseloads of two years earlier, when welfare recipients were more numerous, federal payments were relatively generous.

To be sure, a small number of for-profit firms, specializing in human services consulting and management, have been around for years. The Welfare Reform Act gave them a huge boost. But it also laid out a red carpet for new entrants, including EDS, Deloitte & Touche, and Lockheed Martin Information Management Systems (a division of the parent defense contractor). In competing for contracts under the new system, these companies offered deep pockets, apparent management acumen and almost guaranteed results.

Local governments, meanwhile, needed to act swiftly. Under tight federal guidelines, which their legislatures often made tighter, they began to look beyond their traditional circle of nonprofit providers to meet the need. The private sector was ready, and the public sector was hungry.

Before long, private firms were expanding their roles in this line of business, alone and in concert with nonprofits. Their contract billings to the public sector surged, and their presence in the human services marketplace extended to nearly all the 50 states. Today there are perhaps a few dozen national or regional corporations with extensive, eight- and nine-figure relationships with state and local human service programs. Dozens more are entering the marketplace every month.

Companies offered deep pockets, apparent management acumen and almost guaranteed results.

The very idea of government service delivery has increasingly come under the nationwide spell of privatization.

Along the way, the very idea of government service delivery, even beyond the confines of the traditional welfare program, has increasingly come under the nationwide spell of privatization. In principle, of course, the idea of privatization is as open to nonprofit contractors as to for-profit ones, and there remain branches of the human services where nonprofits continue to dominate. But these branches are becoming smaller and fewer as time goes on and budgets contract.

Few nonprofits have the capital, computers, speed or skill sets to compete directly for the big, omnibus contracts. For example, late in 1997, Dade County, Florida, chose Lockheed Martin IMS to run its multi-million-dollar welfare-to-work program. The first eight-month contract was worth more than $15 million alone. It covered 14,000 people, three-quarters of the welfare recipients of the county. To do this work—day care, drug abuse counseling, job training and mental health services—Lockheed hired more than two dozen local agencies. Some are nonprofit, some are commercial.[5]

Two years later, Lockheed won the lion's share of Washington, D.C.'s welfare-to-work business, too—a $33 million contract. In Washington, D.C., in Miami–Dade County, and in numerous other places around the country today, nonprofits now find themselves working for commercial enterprises as subcontractors, not as partners with government. They are increasingly accountable to business. They have a bottom line and performance goals to meet.

This is a historic and, I think, irrevocable shift. And for a long time, foundations were largely oblivious to it.

ADAPT OR DIE

Confronting the matter now as a *fait accompli*, it would be easy to throw up our hands in despair. It would be a gross overreaction—though not exactly unheard of— to pronounce these trends a death knell for civil society and a sell-off of public responsibility to corporate control. In reality, it is still possible to adapt to the new circumstances and to maintain our place in this increasingly competitive marketplace. But it will not be easy.

Our influence will be determined by our ability to master four significant tasks: accessing capital, using information technology, working at scale, and attracting and keeping the best employees.

Start with access to capital. For-profit corporations can raise money to bid on almost any business they choose and accept a high level of risk. This is important, since contracts increasingly demand that bidders pay for cost overruns.

Most contracts are large and multi-faceted. Successful bidding may mean having to open new offices, pay salaries for months before reimbursements arrive, and meet unforeseen startup costs. In Washington, D.C., Lockheed had three weeks to put together a welfare-to-work office to

Our influence will depend on four significant challenges: capital, technology, scale and talent.

serve 5,000 clients.[6]

For-profits can go to the financial markets to raise working capital. Public companies in the human services market have raised millions of dollars this way. Nonprofits don't have this option. They are constrained by their 501(c)(3) status, which forbids distribution of profit—or even making it. They can't raise capital in exchange for stock; they have none. Many would choose not to, even if they could. High finance is foreign to the nonprofit culture. It is often seen as a distraction from getting the job done.

But, in truth, whether nonprofits are intrigued or repelled by the prospect of corporate-style capital formation, the choice isn't really theirs to make. Dollars simply aren't available to nonprofits to take on additional financial risk or aggressively expand service boundaries.

Yet this is what the Welfare Reform Act virtually demands—and it is one of the act's great accomplishments. It compels local government to break free from destructive, artificial funding silos. After two decades of effort and no real progress, the goal of "service integration" may now be within reach. Transportation, childcare, welfare eligibility, job training and food stamps must now be linked. This is a huge win for beneficiaries in the system.

Many nonprofits haven't the money or capacity to deliver comprehensive services. It's not surprising that entrepreneurial nonprofits are looking for ways to merge, joint venture, be bought out or set up for-profit subsidiaries.

Second, access to information technology, or IT, is critical. It enables providers to operate at sufficient scale and detail to provide all these connected services. This includes the most mundane activities, like bookkeeping and keeping case histories. It involves complicated tasks, too, like calibrating payments to several family members in their transition off welfare.

Increasingly, IT capacity will separate the successful vendor from the mere survivor.

The new Welfare Reform Act mandates pulling together numerous strands of client information. They often are kept separately, in different agencies, at different levels of government, often with different computer systems and protocols. Again, the resource problem emerges. Few nonprofits— and not all that many for-profits—have the funds to buy and use the IT systems needed to manage thousands of clients.

More than hardware and software is involved. Skilled personnel are also necessary. These individuals, always in high demand, command high salaries. Increasingly, IT capacity will separate the successful vendor from the mere survivor. Conversely, its absence will likely mean a loss of autonomy and power.

Many nonprofits invest only a minuscule amount of their overall budgets in IT. Many haven't the staffing expertise to use it expansively. And both commercial and nonprofit providers are having a tough time making IT work in welfare reform. Yet we are in an unforgiving environment. The ability to aggregate and manipulate vast amounts of data (and money) is *the* bottom line. In this competition, many nonprofits will not easily deliver what is required.

Third, welfare reform requires building large-scale operations. Size permits economies of scale across vast service areas. It lets organizations implement master contracts. It offers the ability to aggregate and report on trend data and effectiveness. Maybe most important, it reduces headaches for government servants. Large contracts let government officials rely on others to bundle and oversee their welfare-to-work responsibilities.

Here lies the greatest challenge for small-scale, community-based organizations. They have often dominated service delivery among nonprofit organizations. They will find it hard to stand alone. Yet they are the ones closest to their customers, and they may resist professionals coming in from the outside. Many will need to make common cause with business or with larger nonprofits to survive.

The size and scale question also raises a final concern: *attracting and retaining the best employees.* The issues here are cultural and personal.

In the Washington, D.C., welfare-to-work contract won by Lockheed, the company receives fees pegged to the length of time the client holds a job: $500 on placement, $500 after three months and

Many small-scale community organizations will have to make common cause with business or with larger nonprofits.

84

$1,000 more after six months. Such "pay-for-performance" requirements are growing in frequency. This runs counter to traditional partnerships between government and nonprofits paid through lump-sum contracts. The new arrangements epitomize a "managed care" approach to human services. Some nonprofits will need to undergo a huge cultural shift toward measurement, with rewards based on productivity.

Ultimately, incentives raise the issue of individual compensation. Obviously, it's hard to compete if you don't have the best people. Business may offer superior compensation packages, looser work rules and bureaucracy, bonuses based on performance, even stock options. With increasing frequency, they attract accomplished public and nonprofit executives eager to break free from stifling work rules and inadequate—or perverse—rewards for performance.

I believe nonprofits can still maintain a very significant role. If nonprofits can work out joint ventures with richer, bigger for-profits—or even nonprofits—everyone could win. Business could apply its technology and management tools. It could (and does) actually upgrade the skills of non-profit subcontractors and let them do what they do best: one-on-one, personal involvement and steady care.

A prototype for this occurred in the late 1990s between Lockheed and the Urban League chapter in Baltimore, around child-support enforcement and family reunification. The Urban League did the skills training and placement for custodial parents. Over nearly three years, President Roger Lyons said, "we've placed more than 1,000 people." He was bullish on his relationship with Lockheed, which, he said, "not only upgraded our staff's skills.... We also helped *them* work better with state officials and the public." This is a model worth developing.

We must avoid trashing the evolving system before it really has a chance to kick in.

We are coming out of a system that for decades treated welfare recipients terribly. The grim view of the private sector as amoral profit maximizers, out to cream the system, obscures a core fact: The public and nonprofit sectors have only spotty records of success themselves. They surely can't claim the entire high road.

We must avoid trashing the evolving system before it really has a chance to kick in. In fact, we need to keep pressing for improvements. If we don't help build its capacity and resiliency, the results could be as cruel as our current, rudderless health care non-system.

Restoring Balance and Accountability: An Update (circa 2006)

Over the next few years, the nonprofit community will face a series of challenges and obstacles. Our mission, our goals, even our identity, will evolve in unpredictable ways. But we can, and must, continue to assist the disadvantaged, the historically abandoned, the ignored.

So between those firm challenges and the flux of a changing marketplace, what is the role of philanthropy? Foundations must support improved management and benchmarking by nonprofits—an area of chronic underfunding that becomes more perilous as today's new demands mount. Service outcomes should be researched and made public. Poor results should be identified and fixed. We should help nonprofits compete where possible, and to link up with others, nonprofit or for-profit or both, when desirable. This is an urgent need if we are to demonstrate, in more than rhetoric, that nonprofit service providers can continue to "deliver the goods."

We should help nonprofits compete where possible and link up with others when desirable.

Foundations and our nonprofit colleagues together can aggressively call for public policy that delivers what it promises. We can press for increased accountability by state and local governments, and the private sector as well. It is in our own interest to keep government open and responsible, and to foster high standards for assisting people coming off welfare—adults and children alike.

Finally, we must be willing to ask—and answer —some other hard questions. Among them are: What constitutes a nonprofit organization? What gives it its special status, different from for-profit vendors? Can a state or locality withdraw its tax exemption from the same group it has asked to provide services? Can a service deliverer advocate for changes in the services it is under contract to deliver? Where does the service end and the advocacy begin?

What can we do to improve the skills and concerns of government regulators and contractors? How can we develop standards and regulations that prevent destabilizing competition and ensure our dollars will be well spent and on those who need it. Does the "devolution" of human services need the brakes put on?

These questions can't be answered with any confidence today, but they need to be raised soon. And philanthropy is well behind schedule in seeking, testing and discussing what the answers might be. There is still time to find those answers and to make the most of what is, for now, still a troubling but salvageable situation.

This little reflection was originally meant solely to help the Surdna Foundation's Board weigh the pros and cons of allowing our staff to serve on grantees' boards—a practice that has become increasingly common within the Foundation, even as it stirred up the occasional dust-storm of controversy in other places.

Reflecting on my memo a year or so later, I realized that the issues weren't really peculiar to our Foundation at all, but have to do with an issue that affects the quality of philanthropy and the management of non-profit organizations writ large. In short, the question is: How do grantmakers get to know the real world of nonprofit management and practice if they wall themselves off from the board rooms where the real problems are confronted and resolved?

I conclude that board service is part of a grantmaker's continuing education and an important contribution, beyond dollars, to the success of our grantees. But even those who come to a different answer might find the issues raised in this memo provocative.

For Funders Trying to Grasp the Realities
of Nonprofit Life—a Postscript:

Should Foundation Officers Serve on Their Grantees' Boards?

IRS reg.§ 53.4941 (d)-2(f)(2): A foundation's grant to a public charity 'will not be an act of self-dealing merely... because one of the [public charity's] officers, directors or trustees is also a manager of or a substantial contributor to the foundation.'

Adapted from a memo to the Surdna Foundation Board of Directors, September 26, 2006, published with the Board's permission.

Just because a foundation's grant to an organization with which it shares a board member is not
necessarily an act of self-dealing, however, does
not make it something the foundation should
undertake without due consideration. Many
foundations have policies that require the relevant board member to abstain from voting on
the grant, and some further bar him or her from
participating in discussions of the proposed grant.
At a minimum, all foundation board members
should be made aware of any colleague's special
interest in the grant.

*There are real
benefits that derive
from grantmakers'
service on grantees'
boards.*

— *Council on Foundations,*
Council Columns, *June / July 2004*

Many people in and around philanthropy feel
that foundation program officers (and CEOs and
board members) should not serve on the boards of
organizations they support. The primary reasons are
(a) that this kind of joint service holds either the
appearance or the reality of conflict of interest and
(b) that the foundation should not "play favorites"
in any manner.

In practice, conflicts of interest, whether a matter of appearance or reality, are not common at the
larger foundations. I have never seen one directly,
though I am sure it occasionally does happen (and
apparently did in the case of the J. Paul Getty Trust,
for example). Still, the argument fails to grasp the
real benefits—both to the grantee and to the foundation staff and board—that derive from grantmakers'
service on the boards of grantee organizations.

The positives far outweigh the negatives.

Regarding the first objection: No single institution (with the possible exception of the Bill and Melinda Gates Foundation) contributes so much money as to have such a decisive impact on grantees, except for the smallest. Think about it. Would a grant of $100,000 or $200,000 or more, or the promise of it, cause a grantee that's strong enough to deserve such a contribution to materially change its policies or program directions to follow the funder's wishes? Not likely. And responsible boards would strongly resist the pressure.

At Surdna, program officers sit on boards of the organizations they support to learn and to help their grantees "beyond the money." These organizations have been tabbed as winners by the Foundation, and there is much sense in continuing to do everything reasonable to help the nonprofit succeed further.

But the benefits run both ways. As board members, program officers can *learn* more about (a) the programs they fund, (b) the condition of organizations in their field, and (c) the way boards actually work. Not the least, they can also return the favor by (d) providing critical assistance. Each of these benefits warrants explanation.

Learning About Programs. Nothing is as presumptuous and dangerous as program staff thinking they know their subject more and better than grantees. Working in a foundation is hermetic. When

As board members, program officers can *learn* more about the programs and organizations they fund.

speaking to funders, people shave the truth all the time. Getting a realistic understanding of day-to-day activities and programmatic implementation makes staffers far more knowledgeable about the issues facing a specific grantee and other, similar grantees in the field. But that kind of knowledge is unlikely to come, uncensored and unvarnished, from the usual grantee–funder interactions. Program officers who work with one or more grantees from the inside will be smarter grantmakers the next time around and thus do their job better.

Learning About Operations. Many program staff know almost nothing about how their grantee organizations actually function. They are trained to look at program development and implementation. Further, it's virtually impossible to know the financial and personnel situation of a grantee without being on the inside. With a board seat, an officer not only sees the difficulties up close, but has a chance to be directly helpful and to head off major problems. More broadly, it's a chance to consider how one's grantmaking can be helpful — or harmful — to organizations struggling for stability and effectiveness. Of course, that kind of insight isn't guaranteed. But, at a minimum, board service broadens grantmakers' experience and improves their sense of how work actually gets accomplished. That, in turn, can't help but improve their grantmaking.

Learning About Boards. Knowing how boards do their business (apart from their own foundation's

> Many program staff know almost nothing about how their grantee organizations actually function.

board, about which most program officers know very little anyway) widens the appreciation and sophistication of staff. The knowledge is invaluable. It makes them better board members of the grantees and better staff members for their own employer. They may well be able to interact with their own board members more intelligently and sensitively, too.

Providing Critical Assistance. Program staff, knowing more about the groups on whose boards they serve, can assist the groups in a variety of ways: in identifying new fund-raising possibilities, in interpreting the foundation community's behavior toward the grantee, in deciding on the "best" strategy, in selecting and assessing the CEO, etc. In the nonprofit community, such assistance is enormously difficult to obtain (especially free) and can sometimes even be the difference between success and failure of the organization. I have never seen program officers be anything less than enthusiastic and diligent in seeking to aid the organizations on whose boards they serve. And if, in the best case, program officers are successful in helping the grantees on whose boards they sit — say, by helping to get a matching grant or identifying a terrific consultant — isn't that precisely their job?

Now for the second objection: Does choosing to sit on a grantee's board show favoritism among the portfolio of grantees? Yes, in a strictly literal sense, it does. But stating the case in that blunt way implies some kind of harm, or at least second-class

Does choosing to sit on a grantee's board show favoritism? And if so, is there any harm in it?

status, being visited on those groups that don't have a foundation representative on their board.

The usually unspoken truth is that all program staff have their "more important" and "less important" grantees, and everyone knows it. Some get more time and attention, some less. Grantees understand that dynamic. In truth, most of them would not relish an intensive, time-consuming relationship with every single grantmaker who gives them support. Service on a group's board is usually not perceived as a zero-sum game by grantees, nor should it be.

Finally, it's important to note that serving on nonprofit boards is becoming increasingly common. This is especially true in the case of "venture philanthropists" who, as a matter of course, ask for and get board seats. Plenty of distinguished organizations have such funders represented on their boards—including Teach for America, College Summit, Jumpstart, Harlem Children's Zone, and various museums and performing arts organizations, among others. In the future we can expect to see more of this engagement, not less.

Two important steps can help to ensure that board service is entirely constructive and within the bounds of both ethics and effective grantmaking.

First, program staff should not be permitted to serve on boards in such a way that they falter in doing their foundation job. Good board service is sometimes time-consuming, and there are limits to how much time can be spent. From my experience, a program officer should not serve on more than two working boards (not counting committees that serve the field directly, such as collaborative bodies and affinity groups). Some boards require little time. It is the job of the senior staffer or CEO to track their staff members' obligations and time commitments and handle any problems (including conflicts) that may occur.

The keys are disclosure and transparency.

Second, all transactions at both the foundation and the grantee organization should be as transparent as possible. There are gradations of participation. Program staff should make their involvement with grantee organizations known within the foundation whenever any transaction involves personal, extra commitment, including board service. It is an open question whether they need to recuse themselves when votes are taken, though doing so is probably prudent. The keys here—as always—are disclosure and transparency.

FOOTNOTES FOR
HIGHER VALUES, BOTTOM LINES

[1] "Should Nonprofits Seek Profits?" by Jeffrey Bradach and
William Foster, *Harvard Business Review*, February 2005.

[2] "Profits for Justice," by Michael H. Shuman and Merrian Fuller,
The Nation, January 24, 2005.

[3] White House press release, "President Highlights Faith-Based
Initiative at Leadership Conference," March 1, 2005.

[4] Cited in *The World of the High Holy Days*, edited by Jack Riemer,
loose leaf, p. 70.

[5] William P. Ryan, "The New Landscape for Nonprofits,"
Harvard Business Review, January 1999, p. 132.

[6] Audrey Rowe, then senior vice-president of Lockheed-Martin
IMS, personal communication, February 17, 1999.

3

'To Strengthen the Bonds Among Us'

Thoughts on nurturing civil society,
citizenship and the public sphere

These remarks provide a platform for the broader theme running through this last section: that the future of philanthropy, volunteerism, nonprofits — the whole complex enterprise we think of as civil society — depends most of all on a prevailing ethic of common responsibility for the common good. Strengthen that ethic, and philanthropy, community and society all thrive. Undermine it, and not only does the work of philanthropy count for less and less, but the society as a whole begins to unravel. This is hardly some new insight of mine — it dates back centuries.

My little contribution, summed up here and in the excerpts that follow, is that we stand at a moment of both enormous opportunity and great peril in our civic life. Philanthropy and civil society, if they work together ambitiously, might be able to tip the balance for the good. If they don't, it's becoming fairly clear which way it will tip on its own.

from

Philanthropy's Role in Building an Effective Citizenry

Opening remarks at the inaugural conference 'PACE — Philanthropy for Active Civic Engagement,' New York City, May 2, 2005.

Have you ever heard of the Ephebic Oath? This is the oath of citizenship taken by young men, aged 18–20, in the city-state of Athens in the 4th century B.C. Each had to pass a two-year course covering military practice and civic duties. At the end of the first year, these teenagers were given a spear and a shield. Then each took this oath:

> We will never bring disgrace on our City by an act of dishonesty or cowardice.

We will fight for the ideals and sacred things of the City both alone and with many.

We will revere and obey the City's laws, and will do our best to incite a like reverence and respect in those above us who are prone to annul them or set them at naught.

We will strive increasingly to quicken the public's sense of civic duty.

Thus in all these ways we will transmit this City, not only not less, but greater, better and more beautiful than it was transmitted to us.[1]

For its time and place, the Ephebic Oath was the rough equivalent of our Pledge of Allegiance. It's an amazing statement—the way it balances individual and group action; how it blends pride and humility; its respect for the law and reverence for a culture that made the law possible; its regard for history; the responsibility it imposes to convey the state in better shape than when it was found.

Fiorello LaGuardia, New York City's mayor in the 1930s and '40s and a true social capitalist, knew this oath well. He spoke of it often, and publicly vowed to follow its precepts. Some say LaGuardia asked his commissioners to pledge to it too, as he handed them their responsibilities. (He probably didn't.)[2] For us who care deeply about democratic participation and civic health, the oath has much to say today.

> For us who care about democracy and civic health, the Ephebic Oath has much to say.

99

THE BAD NEWS

Most everyone agrees we're in a civic mess. Despite a spike in voting patterns at the beginning of the century—from 54 percent in 2000 to 59 percent in 2004, the highest turnout since 1968[3]—the challenges seem even larger than when Robert Putnam published his sobering article "Bowling Alone," in 1995,[4] on which his book of the same title was later based.[5] In fact, he re-confirmed this view toward the end of 2004 in a speech at the National Conference on Citizenship. His words seem to me plaintive and almost sorrowful.[6]

In the 'Dot-Net' Generation, nearly 6 in 10 are completely disengaged from civic life.

No one disputes anymore the decline of social capital. Political participation has been in a 40-year slide. Volunteering hours are down, though the number of volunteers is up. As Michelle Nunn notes, the time spent in sustained and deep commitment fell 10 percent, to less than four hours per week.[7] As well, trust in government by all Americans has fallen by 50 percent over the last four decades, from 73 percent in 1958 to 36 percent in 2003.[8]

As if this weren't enough, the data are most upsetting with regard to young people. To cite but two of many examples, CIRCLE (the Center for Information and Research on Civic Learning and Engagement), through its Civic Engagement Index, has pinpointed the apathy of the "Dot-Net" Generation, ages 15–25. Nearly 6 in 10 are completely disengaged from civic life. Only 24 percent follow government and public affairs "very often."

Fewer than 4 in 10 say citizenship entails special obligations.[9]

An equally depressing new survey of young people, titled "The Future of the First Amendment" (a survey of more than 100,000 high school students, 8,000 teachers, and 500 administrators and principals in 544 high schools), concludes that civic basics aren't being taught. It shows that nearly three-quarters of the students either don't know how they feel about the First Amendment or take it for granted.[10]

So, if adults are disengaged and apathetic, most every survey tells us that young people are largely turned off. Politics, political parties and government have little or no relevance in their lives. If they choose to participate at all, they see volunteering in nonprofit organizations as the meaningful alternative.

But before we hang it all up and turn off the lights, before we give up on the goals of the Ephebic Oath, we need to ask if there are any data that might give cause for optimism. I will argue, in a moment, that there are. I also want to make two related points. The first is that philanthropy can do a lot better in building an engaged citizenry. The second is that the federal government, in the first decade of the new century, has pulled us in two very different directions at the same time: One direction holds the promise that the civic engagement of the nonprofit sector, often spurred on by government funds, can flourish. The other direction, however, will so degrade civic engagement that lasting damage will be done.

THE GOOD NEWS

The picture of civic ignorance and popular withdrawal hung over my head as I thought about what philanthropy can do to build civic engagement. In two places, I found cause for optimism about how philanthropy could make a difference. One is the practice of *funding direct action to create a broader social change movement.* This approach, supported by some foundations, is a feature of our grantmaking. It enlists citizens in envisioning and achieving a better society, by calling forth their energies to rearrange current systems and practices. Surdna offers a very strong example of such efforts.

The other is what I would characterize as *"pure service."* To me that connotes efforts to cultivate an ethic of personal service to others, addressing private needs, where government is a major player. Here, changing or making policy is not the goal; it's meeting needs right now. The two approaches are complementary.

I reviewed more than a decade of Surdna grantmaking, which has totaled more than $350 million between 1990 and 2004. What I found surprised me. The thematic coherence around civic engagement was remarkable. In rough numbers, Surdna has made more than 1,000 grants, totaling well over $100 million, in support of civic engagement. A large

By funding direct action for social change, philanthropy can enlist citizens in achieving a better society.

majority of these grants have followed the charge given us by Harry Boyte and Nan Kari, in their important 1996 book, to do "public work."[11] We've done it all over America, often with great consequence.

Here's a brief sample of six Surdna projects and what they accomplished. The point of listing them is not to illustrate the brilliance of our own grant-making. The point is to show the range of opportunity for a committed foundation to delve deeply into this line of work. Most of these grants, in fact, were made collaboratively with other foundations.

Start with the most basic form of common wealth: land. Nationally, we've supported local land trusts that arrange for conservation easements, or the outright acquisition of property, for the public good. There are now more than 1,500 of them. About half are run by volunteers. The total acreage conserved by land trusts more than doubled between 1998 and 2003, to 9.4 million acres.[12] That's almost double the land mass of New Jersey.

Second, in Los Angeles, the Labor/Community Strategy Center has been our partner for a decade. Through its Bus Riders Union, LCSC has fought for 12 years for a modern and efficient bus system for 400,000 low-income bus riders in the city. This system is their lifeline — for employment, education, recreation and family. Yet the Los Angeles transportation authority wanted to shrink it drastically, and raise fares, which would have made regular

There are many ways for a committed foundation to delve deeply into this line of work.

travel both uncertain and unaffordable. LCSC took the authority to federal court. It won a landmark civil rights consent decree that compelled the MTA to improve the bus system and make it its first priority in funding. Now, under a 10-year contract, overseen by the Bus Riders Union, hundreds of millions of dollars in improvements are being pumped into low-income, mass-transit–dependent communities.

Third, in 1992, Surdna created a seven-year-long, comprehensive community revitalization program. It covered a large section of the South Bronx. It was run by five community development corporations representing thousands of neighborhood residents. We bought into *their* plans. Twenty-one funders, banks and the city government provided more than $12 million and assisted the CDCs in raising about $44 million more. Numerous health, employment and economic development programs were set up.[13] This collaborative model has spread to other cities, like Chicago.

Fourth, the Ella Baker Center and the Youth Justice Coalition, two organizations in California, helped build a coalition of 55 community and youth-serving nonprofits. Many of the groups in the coalition are run by young people. They have compelled the state to completely reform its horrific treatment of young people in California's juvenile-justice system. Their work has forced the California Youth Authority to stop placing young people in

A coalition of 55 community groups, many led by young people, has driven a juvenile-justice reform in California.

adult facilities and to ensure that kids who are pepper-sprayed in the course of law enforcement get legally mandated medical treatment within 15 minutes. Because of their actions, youth now sit on committees that review discipline and grievance procedures. Under mounting citizen pressure, in December 2004 the governor agreed to a systematic overhaul of California's entire juvenile detention apparatus.

Fifth, in technology, one of our many projects has been to help fund the start-up of YouthNoise. This website now engages more than half a million young people a month. More than half the content on the site is actually created by these young users. Large numbers use it to find volunteer work, to engage in online policy debates and to contact legislators to express their concerns.

Finally, we've been one of many supporters and advocates of the Rails-to-Trails Conservancy. RTC is the only national group devoted to preserving abandoned railroad corridors by converting unused rail lines to multi-use trails for everybody, for walking, exercising, etc. RTC has catalyzed the preservation and building of more than 1,100 rail trails covering 12,000 miles of open trail.

All these efforts have a special, similar footprint. They are issue-based, place-based and usually *locally focused*. Most are overtly "political" in the sense that they mobilize citizens to envision a better world, create change and, when necessary, take on

A real fire is burning under the civic engagement embers many of us have written off as nearly extinguished.

government. They navigate the messy democratic process of sifting and sorting competing interests. They *take action* to fix lòcal problems.

You can be sure that none of the participants thought they were building social capital, let alone rescuing democracy. But these nonprofit groups, and thousands like them, exist in countless places — rural, suburban and urban. They give a strong and clear message: A real fire is burning under the civic engagement embers many of us have written off as nearly extinguished.

Something important is going on here. It's about what the Ephebic Oath calls "fighting for the ideals and sacred things ... both alone and with many."

E. J. Dionne and Kayla Drogosz have written:

> Public work entails not only altruism, but also enlightened self-interest — a desire to build a society in which the serving citizen wants to live. Service alone cannot build a stronger sense of citizenship. Citizenship is meaningless unless citizens have the power to achieve their goals and to change their communities and the nation.[14]

PRIVATE ACTS, PUBLIC ACTION

Now what about the second category, "pure service"? The first category featured nonprofits that deliberately focus on training individuals to do or to practice broad-based civic improvement. They often address a need when the public system has failed. Here, the reverse is the case; government is a supporter of this kind of service, not an antagonist. The work is often individualized, from visiting an elderly citizen to serving food in a soup kitchen. In its reach, this approach is enormous.

Many of the nonprofits doing this work are funded by AmeriCorps. There are several thousand of them. They are forbidden by law to engage in politics if they take AmeriCorps money. Some get foundation grants too. Among these nonprofits are national organizations like City Year, Public Allies, Teach for America and YouthBuild.

I believe pure service is an important part of the mix. Some of our colleagues have dismissed this approach as episodic and too divorced from the political fray to have much civic meaning. But I think we can't react so skeptically.

For here, we can say without hesitation that these groups are producing engaged citizens. While the data are just coming in, the story here is remarkably positive — especially for young people.

For example, the first rigorous, scientific study of alumni of AmeriCorps came out in 2005, released by the Corporation for National and Community Service, which administers AmeriCorps. It covered more than 2,000 randomly selected former AmeriCorps members. It finds that:

> Effects of participation were especially strong in the area of civic engagement.... There were statistically significant increases in: members' connection to community, knowledge about problems facing

'Pure service' groups are producing engaged citizens with remarkably positive results.

their community, participation in community-based activities [like attending public meetings and writing to newspapers] and personal growth through service.[15]

This is good news, and more research is under way. Since AmeriCorps' inception, more than 380,000 men and women have gone through the program. Their average age is in the early 20s.

There's more. Public Allies has found that almost 60 percent of their alumni continue their careers in public service. More than half of them work in education and youth development, and they volunteer twice as much as a comparison group. They vote at a level of more than 90 percent and retain a deep interest in public affairs.[16]

As I write this, City Year is completing three independent studies, and early indications are that continued, deeper civic engagement has happened among its graduates.

As of 2005, Teach For America had more than 9,000 alumni. More than 60 percent were still working in education and more than 90 percent of those are working in low-income communities. In that same year, TFA got a record 17,000 applications for 2,000 slots—a 39 percent increase over 2004.[17]

YouthBuild, which engages disadvantaged young people, produced strong numbers, too. In a survey of 900 of their 27,000 graduates over a 12-year period, they found that 68 percent vote regularly and 48 percent still participate in community

Alumni of Public Allies vote at a level of more than 90 percent.

organizations or do voluntary work. Fourteen per cent serve on community councils or neighborhood boards.[18]

Something important is going on here too. It's about what the Oath describes as "striving increasingly to quicken the public's sense of civic duty."

I don't for a minute pretend to have discovered a movement that all of us had somehow overlooked. But I do believe that we can connect the dots of these and other efforts. If we do, we will sense a true counterweight to the sour and depressing conventional wisdom about citizen engagement.

Once we start connecting the dots—drawing lines that both link the various branches of civic activity and break down the narrow definitions of our program interests—we will surely be more realistic in our assessments, more accurate in our views, and more effective in our grantmaking. Our glass is a lot fuller than we recognize, and the two approaches to service, properly accounted for, may make up the core of a rebirth of effective citizenry.

I suspect a national network is ready to come alive. But…

GOVERNMENT AS FRIEND, GOVERNMENT AS ENEMY

In 2005 President Bush submitted a budget request to Congress for $921 million for the Corporation for National and Community Service. The request was designed to enable the Corporation to continue supporting 75,000 AmeriCorps members (including

VISTA), as well as participants in the Senior Corps and Learn and Serve programs. The appointed managers of these programs, and of the National Corporation, have been staunch supporters. In a time of severe fiscal stress, as this publication goes to press, the Corporation is once again facing the threat of budget cuts.

So what motivates so much concern about the future of citizen service? It's this: On the macro level, the federal government seemed determined, as of 2005 and beyond, to dismantle other service institutions that our citizens have built, piece by piece, throughout this nation's history. This alone may gravely damage all the good work cited above.

The first source of alarm is the federal budget. Domestic budgets have plunged the country further into debt and restricted aid to families that need it most. In order to provide tax cuts for the top one-half of 1 percent of the population, the president's Fiscal 2006 budget proposed reducing education and training dollars by 14 percent, environment and natural resources by 23 percent, health by 12 percent, with a total domestic discretionary cut of 14 percent—all by 2010.[19] Cuts would be made in entitlement programs as well, including those that provide basic life supports for low-income families, and their number will grow every year. The middle class will feel the pinch too.

The reductions will put yet more pressure on an already overworked and underpaid nonprofit sector.

This administration's unspoken belief that voluntary service organizations and nonprofits can pick up the slack is a dangerous fantasy. As Brian O'Connell, the founding chair of Independent Sector, has written:

> I am a great believer in voluntary initiative, but we make a terrible mistake if we exaggerate what voluntary activity can do, particularly if it allows us to exaggerate what government need not do. The mistake is compounded seriously when citizens sit on the sidelines as cynics and critics of government, forgetting that in a democracy we are the primary officeholders of government.[20]

The belief that voluntary service organizations can pick up the slack for government service cuts is a dangerous fantasy.

My second concern is federal tax policy. To take just one example, the cuts in the estate tax proposed in 2005 would, in the view of the Brookings Institution and the Urban Institute,[21] reduce philanthropic giving by perhaps $10 billion annually.[22] Indeed, the formation of new foundations dipped last year, and the loss to philanthropy will grow as the rich lose their incentive to be charitable. That translates into less money to support civic engagement.

Third is the systematic degradation of government and its public servants. It should be clear by now that the Bush administration did not set out to wring efficiency from a bloated government. It hoped to kill off much of government itself. The way it went about this was to so under-fund federal agencies that they become enfeebled and increasingly ineffectual. When that happens, they can privatize services or kill off agencies completely (like bus service in low-income communities, or the proposed fate of the Department of Housing and Urban Development). And by enfeebling government agencies, the administration signals that it would rather confront than collaborate with citizens' groups.

A policy that belittles public servants not only hurts government and the public it is sworn to serve. It also makes public institutions increasingly unattractive places to work. Why should talented young people enter professions that are systematically ridiculed and shrunken? What kind of an incentive is this for public service? We've seen this trend clearly in the recent, inflammatory calls for the removal of judges. We've seen it in the degradation of the judiciary at all levels. Our judges uphold the culture of law that makes effective citizenship possible. That idea is central to the Ephebic Oath.

Finally, there is the hysterical tone of communication throughout politics and the commercial media. This current wave of shouting and bashing began with the impeachment of President Clinton and has gotten more vicious through two subsequent election cycles, the sad, desperate case of Terri Schiavo, two Supreme Court vacancies, and on and on. How can we foster effective citizenry with this intolerant, even threatening, language that now passes for discourse? This language has even infected members of Congress.[23] Remember the

A policy that belittles public servants not only hurts government and the public, it also makes public institutions increasingly unattractive places to work.

Oath: We "will do our best to incite a like reverence and respect in those above us who are prone
to annul them or set them at naught."

Can we model public participation, especially
for young people, when most of what they see and
hear are politicians so polarized that they tear
down the concept of thoughtful deliberation and
compromise? Can you blame so many young people
for turning away from politics?

A positive, sometimes contentious, connection
between government and its citizens has been
essential throughout the history of this country.
Citizens depend on each other, and on their government, for protection and service, and for some
modicum of respect and recognition. We need to
build this up, not dismantle it. As Theda Skocpol, an
astute observer of American democracy, has written:

> Organized civil society in the United States has
> never flourished apart from active government
> and inclusive democratic politics. Civic vitality
> has also depended on vibrant ties across classes
> and localities. If we want to repair civil society,
> we must first and foremost revitalize political
> democracy. ... Re-establishing local voluntary
> groups alone will not suffice.[24]

Can you blame so
many young people
for turning away
from politics?

There are some
among us who
say that it's only a
matter of time until
the blade swings
toward us.

'To Quicken the Sense of Civic Duty'

So, at a time when government both defends and undermines the fundamentals of civic life, what is the role of philanthropy? Possibly the most important step to take is to claim the high road of citizenship, to speak out and demand the civility, respect and funding that enable an effective citizenry to grow. Here we have a poor record. Foundation leaders, at some risk, have to speak out on critical public issues—not just pay nonprofits to speak and act in their stead.

But speaking out isn't enough. We need to put more of our money where our mouths are. As you heard, we *can* identify strategies that build effective citizens. We must create a countervailing force to these destructive trends. That also means more foundation collaboration and policy engagement.

No other institutions in our society have so much leeway, so much access to information, so much public purpose—and so much need to sustain the elements that make democratic participation possible. We shouldn't forget that philanthropy, too, can be weakened in various ways, by legislation or regulation. There are some among us who say that it's only a matter of time until the blade swings toward us.

Nonprofit organizations, foundations and governments will either recognize the importance of respecting each other and working it out together, or they will fall apart together as well. This is the ugly scenario, one we have to prevent, at least so that we can go back to the ideals of the Ephebic Oath and revive and grow an effective citizenry.

from

Hyperbole, Shrinking Budgets and Government Devolution

Keynote address to the Fourth Annual Convocation of the Funders' Network for Smart Growth and Livable Communities, Minneapolis, Minnesota, April 11, 2003.

I grew up in central Brooklyn, what's called Bedford-Stuyvesant today. I walked to all my schools, starting with P.S. 138. I shopped on Nostrand Avenue, two blocks from home. I went to the movies on Eastern Parkway, took the subway to music lessons at the Brooklyn Academy of Music (now BAM), and caught the bus with my brother and father to see Jackie Robinson and Duke Snider play at Ebbets Field. When I was 10 I got lost in the subway going to the dentist. I wound up in Manhattan, alone and hysterical, saved by a friendly conductor. I didn't get a driver's license till my second year in college. Since then, I have owned a car for a grand total of four years.

I couldn't have existed, nor could my working parents, nor their ailing parents, without the convenient blessings of neighborhood, community and New York City's mass transit system. My experience is obviously uncommon in America. But the story it tells has dramatic applicability today.

Maybe 40 percent of Americans, 125 million, give or take, don't drive. They're either too old, too young, too infirm, too inadequate in language skills or, simply, too poor. They're stuck. They have very limited access to transit and very little mobility.

If you look at the 2000 Census numbers, this huge cohort is growing rapidly. The vast number of elderly, and the high proportion of young people among America's immigrants, ensures their numbers will grow disproportionately large. Yet their isolation from well-paying jobs, or any jobs for that matter, from family and friends and shopping and schools and parks and nature marks them indelibly as second-class citizens. They are unable to access the necessary pleasures promised by their life in America.

This is unhealthy and deeply unfair. Our "dumb growth" weakens social cohesion, distorts economic life and economic opportunity, and compels us to overshoot the carrying capacity of the environment.

The isolation of large numbers of people has

begun to deeply etch the soul of the American dream. But the converse is *also* unhealthy and unfair. That is, the flagrant use of automobiles (Americans, with 4 percent of the population, use 42 percent of the world's gasoline) and the mindless abuse of land, water and air threaten to impoverish even those who *have* mobility. So, whether we are able to get around or not, we can't hide anymore.

No one can say there was a conspiracy to fragment America over the last half-century. What we can say is that metropolitan decentralization and the emptying out of cities happened because of affirmative public policies, huge government subsidies and a genuine desire by people to enjoy the real pleasures of the country, nature and open space.

So, we didn't get here by accident or through conspiracy, and it follows that we needn't be forever stuck in the parking lot of auto-dependency, traffic congestion, lack of access to good jobs and good schools. We needn't put relentless stress on our family structures either. Paradoxically, the bad news is the good news: Americans are finally acknowledging they are *both* the cause and the effect, and our present direction leads only to greater, possibly irreparable damage.

Philanthropy at the Front Lines

For some incomprehensible reason, it's not folks on the center or left who talk about a conspiracy to wreck the American dream. It's folks on the

The emptying out of cities happened because of public policies, government subsidies and genuine market demand.

ideological right. They are raising the voltage of their language and beginning to suggest there's something almost unpatriotic about those of us who believe in smart growth. That's ridiculous and sad. Yet the very shrillness of it suggests that arguments for smart growth have struck a nerve, and are evidently strong enough to raise the blood pressure of at least some champions of unfettered, heedless sprawl.

Even so, we do have to be able to answer the critics' more reasoned arguments.

We've got to acknowledge there is a powerful cultural, social and economic drive among Americans to move outward from cities. There is an entirely rational desire to leave highly taxed, physically dangerous, fiscally starved, socially alienating, politically corrupt urban areas. We can't play fast and loose. We have to address these views fairly and directly, while making our case compelling and entirely reasonable—which it is.

I'm really hung up on this. We in foundations mustn't accept the hot wire of criticism with characteristic aloofness. We can't dismiss critics as cranks, and then refuse to enter the contest of ideas. That's the old strategy of "white-glove" philanthropy that lets others fight our battles for us, not with us. Every chance we have to rebut the nay-sayers is a chance to build our smart growth movement. We have to support analysis, education, advocacy, legislation, and even litigation, when the common

> There is a powerful cultural, social and economic drive to move outward from cities.

good is threatened.

Let's start thinking about pooling grant money for strategic effect. Let's start to "co-create" bold new regional programs with our nonprofit colleagues. Let's find uncommon allies in business and government and forge new alliances.

Since the passage of the Intermodal Surface Transportation Efficiency Act of 1991, more commonly known as ISTEA, and the Transportation Equity Act for the 21st Century, or TEA-21, in 1998, we've begun to use the pocket change these two laws set aside from the highway budget to surprisingly promising effect. The two TEAs set down "the principle that America's metropolitan reality required an integrated, balanced and regionally designed transportation system,"[25] kind of like the one I had in Brooklyn. Their implementation has left much to be desired. But the progress they have made possible is beyond dispute.

We know that smart growth slows decentralization of metro areas, promotes intelligent public re-investment, and enhances access to economic opportunity for all of us. The public gets it. We can actually see some rays of light in the local government tunnel. We should act as if they were sunshine.

There is light, too, at the federal and state levels. Start with Senator Daniel Patrick Moynihan, who died in 2003. He was the true spark for this re-birth of concern for balance and conservation in metropolitan development. This brilliant public intellectual,

Let's start to 'co-create' bold new regional programs with nonprofits, business and government.

a son of Hell's Kitchen and longtime resident of Pindars Corners, a tiny hamlet in Delaware County, New York, was the spiritual and *actual* father of ISTEA. In 1991, as head of the Public Works Committee of the Senate, he stealthily inserted the key language that opened up the highway trust fund to alternative spending approaches. What he began a decade ago is our platform on which to build a smart growth movement.

For the first time, now, we have a small cadre of centrist, savvy governors deeply rooted in their states' ethic. They are committed to linking good government and smart growth. I'm thinking, in the early 2000s, of Mitt Romney of Massachusetts, Jennifer Granholm of Michigan, Edward Rendell of Pennsylvania, Mike Leavitt of Utah, and Jim McGreevey and later Jon Corzine of New Jersey. They are surprisingly pragmatic, gutsy and bi-partisan.

Listen to Governor Granholm's remarks in 2003 to her newly created Michigan Land Use Leadership Council:

> The critical issue isn't the product of just another "ism"—conservatism, liberalism, or Republicanism.... We are gobbling up land at a rate that our population won't support, the land base won't maintain, and that we can no longer tolerate.... It's the product of this fundamental question of whether or not we want to save the splendor of our state for our grandchildren's generation and beyond, while still permitting wise economic growth. [It's] about saving our cities and communities.[26]

For the first time, we have a small cadre of centrist, savvy governors committed to linking good government and smart growth.

It's our job to help these 'governors-with-the-long-view' to build the livable communities of the future.

These sentiments aren't radical, elitist or ideological. They are based on observation, experience and reflection. They have resonance with America. Of course, the smart growth that will follow won't be easy to craft or implement. But Phase Two of our journey—following what began with the National Smart Growth Council, formed by former Governors Christine Todd Whitman of New Jersey and Parris Glendening of Maryland—has now begun. It's our job to help these "governors-with-the-long-view" to build the livable communities of the future.

Lots of political capital is going to be spent by these governors and their staffs, allies, colleagues and … *us*. Lots of financial capital will be spent too. Anyone who supposes that funders have the luxury of standing on the sidelines is dead wrong. Anyone who presumes we should watch a great opportunity erode because of our non-participation is also in error. Anyone who suggests we don't have an honorable, compelling, urgent task to build a movement with all Americans is simply missing the challenge of the decade.

Explorer Ernest Shackleton once said, "Optimism is true moral courage." In these surreal, lean and often frightening times I do think there are real grounds for optimism. They've come to us from unexpected places, in unusual ways, in uncommon times. We can't afford to let the challenge pass us by.

This speech was originally written for an audience from a single state, Connecticut, but its premise is really about all, or at least most, states. It is, at its core, a reflection on the size of our ambitions—all citizens' ambitions—for the improvement of our society. Today, the big questions about domestic and social policy—the great themes of human welfare, equality, enfranchisement and opportunity that were once at the heart of national philanthropy and government—now arise more and more at the state level.

Though neither philanthropy nor state governments are yet accustomed to grappling with these big matters, much less envisioning big solutions to them, I argue here that this unreadiness presents a historic opportunity for philanthropy. That opportunity includes, among many other things, reclaiming the big-thinking roots of our field, and the call to effective citizenship on which all great movements depend.

from

Let's Face the Music and Dance

Ernest Shackleton's expeditions to the Antarctic came at roughly the same time—the early decades of the 20th century—that philanthropy was getting under way in America. Yet today we know far more about his exploits than we do about our own.

Our earliest American philanthropic ancestors—John D. Rockefeller, Margaret Olivia Sage (the widow of Russell Sage), Andrew Carnegie, among others—bequeathed a kind of courage and determination to us, a confidence that we can take on large-scale problems with deeply rooted causes. That

Keynote speech at the Connecticut Council for Philanthropy Annual Meeting, Stonington, Connecticut, May 6, 2004.

we can strategically "leverage" large amounts of local government and private dollars. That we can engage the public sector directly and continuously. That we can speak out for our truest causes. That we can stick with our grantmaking for many years and justly claim the high ground. The strategies are all there waiting for us to use. We need invent nothing.

But there is a second path in American grantmaking that diverges from that of the great original donors—call it "small-thinking philanthropy," literally and figuratively.

Briefly, "small philanthropy" is much more like what we have today, with one stunning exception: the Bill and Melinda Gates Foundation. The "small" work is characterized by fierce institutional independence and an unwillingness to go at root causes, alone or together. (If you want an example of this assertion, just scan the coverage in the *Chronicle of Philanthropy* [April 15, 2004] of philanthropy's tangential, ineffective, uncoordinated response to the national scourge of predatory lending.)

Foundations also work unsystematically. They tilt toward satisfaction for the donor, not significance for community or society. Since there are no mechanisms or incentives to learn and to do better, self-improvement is rarely embraced. Neither market forces nor consumers, nor even government agencies, can compel improvement.

Finally, funders are also scrupulously quiet and

'Small-thinking philanthropy' is characterized by fierce institutional independence and unwillingness to go at root causes.

less than transparent. For years it was standard operating procedure to withhold from the public the
information foundations are required to file in the
IRS Form 990PF (they were required to have a
copy available for public inspection). Only since the
establishment of the nonprofit database GuideStar
(www.guidestar.org), in 2002, is broad public
viewing now possible. But with that broad viewing
has come another disappointment: how poorly
foundations bother to fill them out, and how
perilously close several come to skirting the law.[27]

Big problems are really big, and philanthropy is small in comparison. Yet there are opportunities for big thinking.

CITIZENSHIP AT THE STATE LEVEL

Of course the world is different now from the world
in which Rockefeller and Carnegie made their
mark. It's vastly bigger, more complex, more inter-
connected, more dangerous. Big problems are *really*
big, almost intractable, constantly shifting. And
philanthropic money is vastly smaller relative to
government programs and societal need.

Yet contemplating these two approaches to
philanthropy, big and small, is important, for it gives
us a beacon to sail to, irrespective of the political
weather. Consider, as an example, what that choice of
approaches means in one crucial area of American
social policy: the devolution of once-federal power
to the states.

In a paradoxical way, devolution, combined with
states' shrinking resources, presents a tremendous
opportunity for them, spurred on and assisted by

foundations, to seize the initiative and resume a "big-thinking" approach to the common good. In fact, I'd argue that *the most important governmental trend in America today is the opportunity states now have to seize the reins.*

States have always had great control over their people and property. They control legislative and tax policy, build infrastructure, and, directly or furtively, guide economic development. They have the power to diminish local conflicts (or make them worse) create broad metropolitan growth strategies, and formulate policies that will avoid destructive economic and social development.

(Their increasing control over federal dollars is now apparent—in transportation, welfare eligibility and child care, to name a few. States are now the largest source of spending on children, and state officials increasingly direct the dollars that control how children get health care, what kind of schools they go to, and how far their parent(s) will have to travel to get to their jobs. As one official of a neighboring state wryly said about recent budget cuts in his super-agency, "Yeah, I've only got $3-plus billion to spend this year.")

But to make the most of the states' new opportunity—or maybe, to make anything at all of it—we have to go after the big issues. There are plenty of them to choose from, and foundations are among the best ones to identify them. School readiness for all? The inequities and imbalance in

The most important governmental trend in America is the opportunity states now have to seize the reins.

the tax structure? Whatever the subject, a statewide focus—one that can unite the public, philanthropic and nonprofit sectors, that can galvanize citizen involvement, and that can focus massive creative attention on root causes of fundamental problems —is vital.

The big unknown is what it will take to cause us to identify and sharpen foundations' own joint priorities, so that the *collective* weight of funders and nonprofits can be felt. There is such a vacuum of power right now in many states that collaboration would almost be its own reward.

We can fund the research and build the case for change. But we have to find our public voice, too.

SUSTAINED, INFORMED COLLABORATION

In proportion to the size of the issues to be confronted, we should be willing to advocate for our causes, just like our predecessors. We can fund the research and build the case for change in the state. But we have to find our *public voice*, too.

This means regularly dealing with elected and appointed government officials, including state attorneys general, at meetings, cocktail parties, whatever, constantly interacting with them, learning from them and educating them. It means promulgating codes of ethics and behavior for ourselves and even encouraging (as leaders in Michigan did) whistle blowers to report unlawful foundation behavior. We have to shuck off a natural reluctance toward engaging in things political and the desire to remain isolated and once-removed.

Little of consequence in the agenda of newly empowered states—which their citizens, led by philanthropy, can write—is going to happen until foundations and nonprofits on one side, and foundations and government on the other, are in sustained, *informed collaboration*. This might mean establishing offices in state capitols and better monitoring state legislation and regulation, including setting up liaisons in governors' offices. Foundations and nonprofits are public citizens and public advocates. We have standing in our states, both in the halls of power and among the citizenry. We can exercise our right to be on the playing field, not just in the spectator seats.

Foundations and nonprofits can exercise our right to be on the playing field, not just in the spectator seats.

Finally, we mustn't forget the moral high ground. Lots of people want to claim it, many can't find it, some deny it exists. But from all my work at the Surdna Foundation, the one lesson I have learned is that values count for a lot, and they are at the root of our legitimacy. They are what gives our mission life and what animates our efforts. It's not always easy to find that high ground but, when we do, our power, our "leverage," are greatly increased. That's what makes "big-thinking philanthropy" really, really big.

I conclude this little collection with an exercise in civic draftsmanship: an attempt — with learned and experienced help from many sources — to

formulate what a spirit of active, committed citizenship might entail in the 21st century. The point is not to formulate a token of fealty to state or government.

The point is to reinvigorate the sense of mutual obligation, of shared responsibility for the common good, that President Kennedy and Ted Sorensen engraved upon the American consciousness in the 1960s: asking,

collectively and individually, what we can do for our country.

That commitment is, to me, the soul of philanthropy. It is what motivated philanthropy's pioneers and every great exercise in organized generosity and social progress since then.

from

A Citizen's Oath for America

When I gave the speech quoting the Athenians' Ephebic Oath (excerpted at the beginning of this chapter), the audience included two people with a natural interest, and firsthand experience, in the subject of citizen engagement: former Senator Harris Wofford, a past chief executive of the Corporation for National and Community Service, and John Bridgeland, the founding director of the USA Freedom Corps. After the speech, all three of us had the same thought:

Why is there nothing like this in America today?

Presented at the annual meeting of the National Conference on Citizenship, Washington, D.C., September 19, 2005.

Why shouldn't there be? Especially *for young people*, whose eyes and minds and hearts are surely receptive to the great possibilities inherent in becoming an effective citizen.

Harris had been working on this idea for years. And much before him, our Founding Fathers and other civic leaders in the youthful United States worked on it too.

We can remind young people of the importance and nobility of an active civic life.

In those early years they were concerned that individual rights and mutual responsibility find a proper and honorable balance. We can see now how the latter, mutual responsibility, would become the buckle that held our country together through decades of danger and difficulty.

Ten years after my speech on the Ephebic Oath, organizers of the National Conference on Citizenship asked me to propose a draft of a Citizen's Oath. As I grappled with it, Harris and Bridge, along with former Indianapolis Mayor Steve Goldsmith (the chair, at that time, of the Corporation for National and Community Service) and Ted Sorensen and many young people, joined in the review process.

We imagined this Citizen's Oath would be entirely voluntary—but still, a starting place, an invocation for young people to take as they begin high school. And maybe as they graduate, too. It's for them to shape it, and add to it, and breathe life into it, just as it may, in due course, offer them a constant reminder of the importance and nobility of an active civic life.

A CITIZEN'S OATH

As an American I embrace the responsibilities of self-government.

I pledge to learn and live the principles set forth in the charters that define our freedoms: the Declaration of Independence, the Constitution and the Bill of Rights.

I pledge to keep myself informed about the challenges that face our country and world and to work with others to meet those challenges.

I pledge to assist all persons in need, and thereby strengthen the bonds among us.

I pledge to register and vote when I am of age, in every election in which I am eligible.

I pledge to conduct myself according to the highest standards of civic decency, to foster those standards throughout my community, and to expect them of all public officials.

Through these acts, I commit myself to build a more just, humane and ethical nation, for my own and all future generations.

FOOTNOTES FOR
'TO STRENGTHEN THE BONDS AMONG US'

[1] Marcus N. Tod, *A Selection of Greek Historical Inscriptions*, vol. II, from 403 to 323 B.C., Oxford University Press, 1968.

[2] Personal communication from Thomas Kessner, Professor of History, Graduate Center at the City University of New York and author, *Fiorello H. LaGuardia and the Making of Modern New York*, McGraw Hill, 1989.

[3] Report by the Committee for the Study of the American Electorate.

[4] Robert D. Putnam, "Bowling Alone: America's Declining Social Capital," *The Journal of Democracy*, 6:1, 1995.

[5] Robert D. Putnam, *Bowling Alone: The Collapse and Revival of American Communities*, Simon and Schuster, 2000.

[6] National Conference on Citizenship, Annual Conference, December 3, 2004, Washington, D.C.

[7] "Reinvigorating Democratic Participation and Activating an Engaged Citizenry," second draft, from Independent Sector data at http://www.independentsector.org/programs/research/volunteer_time.html.

[8] "American National Election Study, 1958–2002; *New York Times*/CBS News Polls, July 2003.

[9] "The Civic and Political Health of the Nation: A Generational Portrait," a report by Scott Keeter et al., CIRCLE/The Center for Information and Research on Civic Learning and Engagement, September 19, 2002.

[10] "Future of the First Amendment," a study sponsored by the John S. and James L. Knight Foundation, 2005, also found that half of the young people surveyed think the government can censor the internet, and many do not think newspapers should publish freely.

[11] *Building America: The Democratic Promise of Public Work*, by Harry C. Boyte and Nancy N. Kari, Temple University Press, 1996.

[12] "Private Land Conservation in U.S. Soars," Land Trust Alliance press release, November 18, 2004.

[13] Gerri Spilka and Tom Burns, "Final Assessment Report: The Comprehensive Community Revitalization Program in the South Bronx," The OMG Center for Collaborative Learning, March 1998.

[14] E. J. Dionne, Jr. and Kayla Drogosz, "The Promise of National Service: A (Very) Brief History of an Idea," *National Civic Review*, Winter 2003, p. 25.

[15] *Serving Country and Community: Longitudinal Study of Service in AmeriCorps*, Early Findings, Executive Summary, p. 1, December 2004.

[16] 2004 Public Ally Results, in-house document.

[17] Wendy Kopp, CEO of Teach for America, e-mail, April 11, 2005.

[18] Dorothy Stoneman, CEO of YouthBuild, personal conversation, April 28, 2005. The sampling methodology here was less strong than the others.

[19] Center on Budget and Policy Priorities data, compiled March 30, 2005.

[20] Brian O'Connell, "Citizen Participation and Influence in America: Impressive Performance and Alarming Shortfalls," *Public Integrity*, Spring 2003, vol. 5, no. 2, pp. 159-170.

[21] Jon M. Bakija and William G. Gale, "Effects of Estate Tax Reform on Charitable Giving," report by the Urban-Brookings Tax Policy Center, no. 6, July 2003.

[22] That is roughly the equivalent of all the grants made by the country's 82 largest foundations in 2003. Stephanie Strom, "Charities Are Silent on Loss of the Estate Tax," *New York Times*, April 24, 2005, p. 28.

23 For example, Senator John Cornyn of Texas, who recently said, "I don't know if there is a cause-and-effect connection, but we have seen some recent episodes of courthouse violence in this country... . And I wonder whether there may be some connection between the perception in some quarters, on some occasions, where judges are making political decisions yet are unaccountable to the public, that it builds up and builds up and builds up to the point where some people engage in violence. Certainly without any justification, but a concern that I have." From "Senator Links Violence to 'Political' Decisions," *Washington Post*, April 5, 2007, p. A07.

24 Theda Skocpol, "Unraveling From Above," *The American Prospect*, no. 25 (March-April 1996) or http://epn.org/prospect/25/25-cnt2.html.

25 Bruce Katz, Robert Puentes and Scott Bernstein, "TEA-21 Reauthorization: Getting Transportation Right for Metropolitan America," The Brookings Institution Series on Transportation Reform, March 2003, p. 5.

26 Edited text of remarks to open the proceedings of the Michigan Land Use Leadership Council, March 24, 2003, Michigan Land Use Institute March 27, 2003, internet text.

27 See "Accountability: New Equation For Charities—More Money, Less Oversight," *New York Times*, November 17, 2003, and "Foundations' Tax Returns Left Unchecked," *Boston Globe*, December 29, 2003.

Index

accountability, 31, 38, 49, 86, 87
advocacy, 2, 14, 16, 43, 47, 88, 119
AmeriCorps, 107, 108, 109
Andrews, David J., 64
Angelides, Philip N., 41
Annenberg Challenge, 10
Aspen Institute, the, 75

benchmarking, 87
beyond the money, 91
Bill and Melinda Gates
    Foundation, the, 91, 124
boards of directors, 2, 6, 54–56, 89–91
boards of grantees, foundation
    officers' service on, 92–95
boat-building, 29, 30
Boyte, Harry C., 103
Bradach, Jeffrey L., 70
Bridgeland, John, 129
Brookings Institution, the, 111, 113
budget deficits, 35, 46, 53
Bush, George W., 71, 109, 111

California, state of, 41, 42
capacity, 23, 38, 39, 40, 43, 44, 52, 76, 82,
    83, 86, 117
Carnegie Corporation, the, 14, 24
Carnegie, Andrew, 7, 8, 16, 123, 125
Carr, John L., 17
Center for Effective Philanthropy,
    the, 46, 49, 50
Center for Information and Research
    on Civic Learning and Engagement
    (CIRCLE), 100

Center on Budget and Policy
    Priorities, the, 59
charity, 36, 37, 38, 89
Chronicle of Philanthropy, the, 124
citizen engagement, 98–115, 129
Citizen's Oath, 129–131
citizenship, 97–101, 106, 112, 114, 116,
    123, 125, 129, 130
City Year, 107, 108
civic engagement, 100, 101, 102, 106, 107,
    108, 111
co-creating value, 29, 30, 31
Code of 'Pretty Good Behavior,' 28
collaboration, 12, 19, 38, 39, 40, 52, 114,
    127, 128
College Summit, 94
Common Cause, 15
Community Development Venture
    Capital Association, 72
compensation, 85
competition, for-profit vs. nonprofit,
    81–88
comprehensive community
    revitalization program, 13, 104
Congress, U.S., 7, 49, 109, 112
contracting out, 76
Corporation for National and
    Community Service, 107, 109, 129, 130
Corzine, Jon S., 121
Council on Foundations, the, 34, 58,
    75, 90
critical analysis, 48, 49, 56

data collection and dissemination, 48
devolution, federal, 116, 125
Dionne, E. J., 106

distinguished philanthropy, 34, 36, 38, 40, 44
Donors' Forum, the, 6
Drogosz, Kayla M., 106
due diligence, 19, 38, 40

Edna McConnell Clark Foundation, the, 43
educational reform, 28
Ella Baker Center, 104
Emerson, Jed, 23
Enterprise Foundation, the, 25
Ephebic Oath, 98, 99, 101, 106, 112, 115, 129
exit strategy, 19

Fast Company, 71
favoritism, 93
Fleishman, Joel L., 2
Form 990PF, 125
for-profit companies, competition with nonprofits, 75–88
Foster, William, 70
Frumkin, Peter, 22
Fuller, Merrian, 71
Fund for Immigrants and Refugees, 12
Funders Network on Smart Growth and Livable Communities, 25
funding collaboratives, 25, 26, 27

Gardner, John W., 6, 14, 15
general support grants, 20
geographic isolation, 117–118
Georgetown University, 17
Glendening, Parris N., 122
Goldsmith, Stephen, 130
Granholm, Jennifer M., 121
GuideStar, 125

Harlem Children's Zone, 94
Harvard Business Review, 63, 70
Harvard University, 22, 39
Heron Foundation, the, 41
Hewlett Foundation, the, 23
Holmes, Oliver Wendell, 75
Housing and Urban Development, Department of, 112

Illinois, state of, 12
Independent Sector, 64, 111
information technology, 30, 81, 83
Intermodal Surface Transportation Efficiency Act, 120
International House of Pancakes Theory of Philanthropy, 10

J. Paul Getty Trust, the, 90
Jacobs Family Foundation, the, 41
Joyce Foundation, the, 15, 16
Jumpstart, 94

Kari, Nancy N., 103
Kennedy, John F., 129
Kim, Mark T., 22
knowledge-sharing, 39, 40

Lagasse, Emeril J., 56
LaGuardia, Fiorello H., 99
land trusts, 103
Leavitt, Mike O., 121
Letts, Christine W., 39
Libra Foundation, the, 41
Local Initiatives Support Corporation, the, 25
Lockheed Martin IMS, 79, 80, 81, 84, 85, 86

Los Angeles Urban Funders
  Group, the, 25
Lyons, Roger, 86

managed care, 85
mapping, 11, 28
McCune Charitable Foundation, the, 41
McGreevey, James E., 121
mental models, 47, 54
metrics, 27, 31, 38
metropolitan decentralization, 118, 120
Michigan Land Use Leadership
  Council, 121
Minnesota Council on
  Foundations, 34
Moynihan, Daniel Patrick, 120

Nation, The, 71
National Community Development
  Initiative (NCDI), 25
National Conference on
  Citizenship, 100, 129, 130
networks, 23, 31, 40, 44, 55, 109
New Markets Tax Credits, 72
New Profit, 71
New Ventures, 63, 65, 66, 67, 70
Nielsen, Waldemar A., 17, 48
Nunn, Michelle, 100

O'Connell, Brian, 111
Omidyar Foundation, the, 71
Otto Bremer Foundation, the, 38
outcomes, 23, 26, 32

pay-for-performance, 85
Personal Responsibility and Work
  Opportunity Reconciliation Act
  of (welfare reform), 78–81

Philanthropy for Active Civic
  Engagement, 98
Planned Parenthood Federation
  of America, 64, 65, 66, 67, 68
Pledge of Allegiance, 99
predatory lending, 124
privatization, 76, 77, 80
program officer, role of, 32, 95
program-related investments, 40, 41
Public Allies, 107, 108
public service, 108, 112
public transportation, 103, 120, 126
public–private partnerships, 8
Putnam, Robert D., 23, 100

Rails-to-Trails Conservancy, 105
Reinvestment Fund, the, 11
Rendell, Edward G., 121
research data, 2
Rockefeller Brothers Fund, the, 63
Rockefeller University, 8
Rockefeller, John D., 7, 8, 16, 24, 123, 125
Romney, W. Mitt, 121
root causes, 7, 9, 10, 37, 38, 124, 127
Rosenwald, Julius, 7, 8, 16
Ryan, William P., 39

Sage, Margaret Olivia, 123
Sage, Russell, 123
scale, 8, 16, 21, 37, 38, 67, 69, 81, 83, 84, 123
Schiavo, Terry, 112
self-reflection, 47, 48
Senge, Peter M., 27
service, pure, 102, 106, 107
Shackleton, Ernest, 122, 123
Shore, Billy, 70
Shuman, Michael H., 71

silos, 12, 82
Skocpol, Theda, 113
slot-machine philanthropy, 18, 26,
smart growth, 116, 119–122
social capital, 23, 27, 100, 106
Social Enterprise Alliance, 62, 71
social entrepreneurship, 62–73
Sorensen, Theodore C., 129, 130
South Bronx, 13, 104
sprawl, 11, 119
St. Paul Foundation, the, 38
states, power of, 125, 126, 127
success measurement, 19
Surdna Foundation, the, 1, 2, 3, 13, 22, 24,
    51, 54, 89, 128, 139
system of philanthropy, 18, 20
systems, 27, 52, 57, 71, 83, 102

Teach for America, 94, 107, 108
theories of change, 11, 51
TIAA-CREF, 8
Transportation Equity Act for
    the 21st Century, 120

undercapitalization, 21, 23
United States Conference of
    Catholic Bishops, 17, 18
University of Chicago, 8
Urban Institute, the, 111
Urban League, the, 85, 86

venture philanthropy, 26
Venture Philanthropy Partners, 44
voice of philanthropy, 14, 15, 16, 43, 127
voter turnout, 100

welfare reform, 13, 15, 75, 78, 79, 83, 84
Whitman, Christine Todd, 122
Wofford, Harris L., 129

Ylvisaker, Paul N., 15, 16, 49
Youth Justice Coalition, 104
YouthBuild, 107, 108
YouthNoise, 105

Zagat guide to philanthropy, 28